THI
Skin
/EN

HALOGEN
FAMILY FAVOURITES
RECIPE BOOK

The Skinny Halogen Oven Family Favourites Recipe Book

Healthy, Low Calorie Family Meal-Time Halogen Oven Recipes Under 300, 400 and 500 Calories

A Bell & Mackenzie Publication
First published in 2013 by Bell & Mackenzie Publishing

ISBN 978-1-909855-06-9

A CIP catalogue record of this book is available from the British Library

Disclaimer
The information and advice in this book is intended as a guide only. Any individual should independently seek the advice of a health professional before embarking on a diet. Some recipes may contain nuts or traces of nuts. Those suffering from any allergies associated with nuts should avoid any recipes containing nuts or nut based oils.

Contents

Contents

Contents

Introduction

The halogen oven is a remarkable appliance providing a space saving, economical and affordable way to cook for your family. As well as cooking food beautifully, it can save time compared to a conventional oven (sometimes up to 40% quicker) and there's much less washing up. If you are health conscious and eager to provide you and your family with good balanced meals that stay within daily recommended calorie limits then the recipes in this book will suit you perfectly.

'The Skinny Halogen Family Favourites Recipe Book' sets out 80 delicious, homemade, low calorie, family favourite dishes to prepare in your halogen oven. Each recipe is simple to follow, balanced, based on 4 servings and all fall below either 300, 400 or 500 calories each. If you are following a calorie controlled diet, maintaining your weight or just keeping check on your family's meals, you will find recipes to suit you all. Cooking times are nearly all under 60 minutes with minimal preparation.

Cooking skinny low calorie family meals using your halogen oven couldn't be a simpler way to follow a healthy eating plan. We hope you enjoy all the recipes in this book.

You may also be interested in other CookNation titles in the 'skinny' series listed at the end of this book.

What This Book Will Do For You

The recipes in this book are all low calorie family favourite dishes for four, which make it easier for you to monitor your family's overall daily calorie intake. The recommended daily calories are approximately 2000 for women and 2500 for men.

Recommended guidelines for children aged 5 to 10 are 1800 calories.

Calorie calculated recipes are great if you are following a diet or keeping an eye on your family's calorie intake but please remember that it is important for you and your family to maintain a balanced healthy diet and that children meet their daily calorie intakes per government guidelines.

Broadly speaking, by consuming the recommended levels of calories each day you should maintain your current weight. Reducing the number of calories (a calorie deficit) will result in losing weight. This happens because the body begins to use fat stores for energy to make up the reduction in calories, which in turn results in weight loss. We have already counted the calories for each dish making it easy for you to fit this into your daily eating plan whether you want to lose weight, maintain your current figure or are just looking for some great-tasting easy to prepare healthy halogen oven recipes for all the family.

What is A Halogen Oven?

You may already have a halogen oven or perhaps are contemplating buying one. Either way a brief explanation of this remarkable appliance is worth a little time.

A halogen oven is an electrical countertop appliance which performs the same functions as a traditional oven but can be operated at a fraction of the running cost and results in reduced cooking times.

It uses a powerful halogen bulb, housed in the lid of the unit, to produce radiant infrared heat which, when circulated around the glass bowl of the appliance using a powerful fan, cooks the food evenly and quicker than a traditional fan assisted/gas oven.

Halogen ovens should not be confused with microwave ovens which use radio waves to penetrate food, causing friction between water and fat molecules. This friction provides heat which in turn cooks the food.

Typically a halogen oven can reduce cooking times compared to a conventional oven by 20-30% and sometimes by up to 40%. It is worth mentioning that you should be wary of claims that a halogen oven will cut your cooking times in half. If this is your main reason for buying one you may find yourself disappointed with the results.

Every unit will normally come with a low and high grill rack, tongs, a rack to place the lid of the appliance when adding/ removing food (it becomes very hot) and sometimes an extender ring to increase the capacity of the oven (these can also be purchased separately). For advice on which model best suits your needs, refer to the Which Halogen Oven section later in this book.

What Are The Benefits of Cooking With A Halogen Oven?

Cooking times can be reduced by 20-30% compared to a conventional oven but there are many other advantages to cooking halogen style.

Affordable. Depending which model you choose (more on that later) prices range between $40-$100 or £30-£80. This is a fraction of the cost of a conventional oven.

Economical. As well as the affordable price, halogen ovens are less expensive to run than a conventional oven. Because they are smaller, provide a constant temperature due to the circulation of air and the intense heat of the bulb together with accurate temperature sensors, food cooks in less time, which in turn means less electricity. In addition they heat up very quickly so lengthy pre-heating is generally not needed. However it is worth switching the oven on when you begin recipe preparation so that the oven is ready to go.

Multifunctional. Halogen ovens have many uses. They can roast, grill, bake, steam, defrost and can even make toast and boiled eggs.

Healthy. Halogen ovens work best by circulating heat around the food. The use of the wire racks that are provided with the unit mean that if you are looking for a healthier way to cook your food, any excess fat produced while cooking drains away. Also, cooking with a halogen oven requires less additional oil and fats.

Visible. One of the great advantages of a halogen oven is you can literally see your food cooking. The large glass bowl enables you to check on your food without opening the appliance as you would in a conventional oven.

Self-cleaning. Although you can remove the glass bowl, most halogen ovens will come with a self-cleaning function. This is a pre-programmed function to clean your bowl using water and dish soap/washing up liquid.

Is There Anything My Halogen Oven Can't Do?

Due to their size, there are limitations on the quantity of food you can cook. If you have a dinner party of 10 then perhaps the help of a conventional oven would be advised. Most appliances will comfortably cater for 4-6. For the purposes of this book all recipes serve 4.

Halogen ovens work best by circulating air around the food so if too much is packed into the bowl cooking times will increase. Similarly heavily liquid based dishes such as soups will require longer cooking times than you might expect. Vegetables, particularly root vegetables, can take longer than meat to cook in a halogen oven. Pasta and rice should generally be pre-cooked. Tinned pulses and beans are generally better than dried.

All of the above have been taken into consideration in our recipes so don't worry.

Which Halogen Oven?

As with any new purchase you should consider how you will use your appliance and of course the budget you can afford. If you are buying a halogen oven for the first time or replacing a model, we strongly recommend you spend some time researching customer reviews before parting with your money. There are a number of websites dedicated to halogen ovens which provide very useful comparisons. Amazon's customer reviews are also an excellent resource.

Size. Generally halogen ovens come in 7 litre up to 17 litre capacities. 12 litres are generally the most popular. We would advise opting for a larger capacity model if your budget can stretch as this will allow you to cook for more people if needed.

Lid: The lid of a halogen cooker is what houses the cooking element. It can be quite heavy and the element is extremely hot when the lid is lifted off after cooking. Most models should come with a lid rack which enables you to place the lid on your counter top (otherwise the element would burn the work surface). If your budget can stretch, buying a model that has a hinged lid is easier and safer as it does not detach from the appliance.

Extras. It is worth researching which manufacturers will offer some handy extras. As standard you should get a low and high rack with your appliance but some also offer, tongs, extender rings, recipe books and replacement bulbs. Always check the length of guarantee provided with each model.

Tips

* If your model has an extender ring, consider using it so that the element is further away from your food. For dishes that could potentially splash while cooking, this prevents the element from becoming dirty. The element can be difficult to clean so this will keep things manageable. Always wipe down the element when cooled with a damp cloth after cooking.

* Make sure you have enough space on your counter top. Although halogen ovens are relatively compact if you do not own the model with a hinged lid you will have to allow space to remove the lid onto the lid stand.

* Use foil to prevent food from browning too quickly. This is not always necessary but can be a good way to prevent food from burning. Alternatively the extender ring can serve the same purpose by placing the element further from the food.

* Be prepared to adjust cooking times. Groceries are rarely uniform in size and each model of halogen may be slightly different, so increasing or decreasing your oven temperatures and cooking times may be needed.

* Ensure you have the right size ovenproof dishes and baking trays for your halogen oven before you begin cooking.

* Consider which rack to use – low or high. If you need your food to brown the high rack will be best but if you require longer cooking times use the low rack. All our recipes specify which should be used.

* Lay some tin foil on the base of your bowl to catch any cooking juices. This will make washing up much easier.

* Always read the manufacturer's instructions. These will offer some additional tips and safety guidelines to get the most out of your particular appliance.

All Recipes Are A Guide Only

All the recipes in this book are a guide only. You may need to alter quantities and cooking times to suit your own appliance.

THE Skinny HALOGEN OVEN FAMILY FAVOURITES RECIPE BOOK

Beef, Pork, Lamb

Beef Stew
Serves 4

Calories Per Serving **385**

Ingredients:

Low cal cooking spray
600g/1lb 5oz lean stewing beef, trimmed and cubed
1 tbsp plain/all-purpose flour
100g/3 ½oz lean, back bacon
1 tbsp worcestershire sauce
1 onion, chopped
2 carrots, chopped
2 parsnips, chopped
4 cloves garlic crushed
100g/3 ½oz mushrooms, sliced
1 tsp each freshly chopped thyme & oregano
120ml/ ½ cup red wine
500ml/ 2 cups beef stock
Salt & pepper to taste

Method:

- Brown the beef in a frying pan with a little low cal spray.
- Remove the beef and place in a plastic bag with the plain flour and shake well to cover the meat.
- Meanwhile gently sauté the bacon, onions, parsnips, garlic, carrots and mushrooms in a little low cal spray for a few minutes.
- Season well and add all the other ingredients to the pan.
- Stir well bring to the boil and place in an ovenproof dish.
- Cover tightly, place on the lower rack and leave to cook in the halogen oven at 180C/350F for 60 – 70 minutes or until the beef is tender & cooked through.
- Remove the lid for the last 10 minutes of cooking to reduce the liquid down if needed.

Beef stew is a national institution. Use the best quality stewing steak you can get and don't worry if you don't have red wine, just increase the stock quantities.

FastFood Steak Sandwich

Serves 4

440

Calories Per Serving

Ingredients:

Low cal cooking spray
450g/1lb frying steak, trimmed
1 onion, sliced
½ tsp paprika
50g/2oz mushrooms, sliced
1 red (bell) peppers, sliced
2 tsp worcestershire sauce
4 low fat cheese slices
1 tbsp freshly chopped oregano
Salt & pepper to taste
4 low fat wholemeal sandwich rolls

Method:

- Gently sauté the onions, peppers and mushrooms in a frying pan with the paprika, worcestershire sauce and a little low cal spray for a few minutes.
- Season the steak well, spray with low cal cooking oil and place on the grill pan at the top of the halogen oven on 240C/475F. Grill for 4-5 minutes each side or until the steak is cooked to your liking.
- Allow the steak to rest for a few minutes and then slice as thinly as possible.
- Divide the meat and sautéed onion mixture across the sandwich rolls and place a cheese slice on top.
- Close each sandwich roll over and individually wrap in foil.
- Turn down the halogen to 180C/350F and place the foil wrapped sandwiches on the lower shelf to cook for 4-5 minutes.

Cheese steak sandwiches are wholesome family fast food. You could experiment with marinating the steak before grilling to make it extra tender.

Chilli Con Carne & Tortilla Chips
Serves 4

Calories Per Serving **490**

Ingredients:

Low cal cooking spray
500g/1lb 2oz lean minced beef
400g/14oz tinned chopped tomatoes
300g/11oz tinned kidney beans, drained
1 onion, chopped
120ml/ ½ cup beef stock
120ml/ ½ cup tomato passata/sieved tomatoes
1 tsp each brown sugar, oregano, cumin, mild chilli powder, paprika & garlic
½ tsp salt
125g/4oz tortilla chips

Method:

- Brown the mince, onions and spices in a frying pan with a little low cal spray.
- Combine all the ingredients, except the tortilla chips, into an ovenproof dish.
- Cover and place on the lower rack of the halogen oven on 200C/400F for 50-60 minutes or until the beef is cooked through.
- Leave uncovered to cook for a further 10 minutes to reduce down the sauce if needed.
- Serve with the tortilla chips on the side.

The Spanish name means 'chilli with meat' and this dish has been a Tex-Mex classic since before the days of the American frontier settlers.

Corned Beef Hash Bake

Serves 4

487

Calories Per Serving

Ingredients:

Low cal cooking spray
400g/14oz lean corned beef, cubed
450g/1lb potatoes, peeled and cut into small cubes
125g/4oz chopped white cabbage
75g/3oz peas
1 carrot, finely chopped
1 onion, sliced
Pinch crushed chilli flakes
120ml/½ cup beef stock
Salt & pepper to taste

Method:

- Gently sauté the onions, cabbage, carrots and potatoes in a little low-cal cooking spray.
- Season and combine all the ingredients in an ovenproof dish.
- Place on the lower rack of the halogen oven on 200C/400F for 30-40 minutes or until the vegetables are tender and the stock is absorbed.

Use the best quality corned beef available to reduce the fat content.

Bean & Sausage Bake

Serves 4

Calories Per Serving **414**

Ingredients:

Low cal cooking spray
8 lean pork sausages, sliced
600g/1lb 5oz tinned mixed beans, drained
400g/14oz tinned chopped tomatoes
1 onion, chopped
2 carrots, finely chopped
1 tbsp tomato puree/ paste or ketchup
1 tsp brown sugar
1 tsp dijon mustard
60ml/¼ cup vegetable stock

Method:

- Brown the sausage pieces in a frying pan with the onions and a little low cal cooking oil for a few minutes.
- Combine all the other ingredients in an ovenproof dish and season.
- Place on the lower rack of the halogen oven at 200C/400F for 30-40 minutes or until the sausages are cooked through, the vegetables are tender and the stock is absorbed.

This is a really simple suppertime meal which always goes down a treat with the whole family.

Lancashire Lamb Hotpot

Serves 4

475

Calories Per Serving

Ingredients:

Low cal cooking oil spray
500g/1lb 2oz lean lamb fillet, cubed
2 onions, chopped
4 carrots, chopped
25g/1oz plain/all-purpose flour
1 tbsp worcestershire sauce
500ml/2 cups lamb stock
1 tbsp tomato puree/paste
1 bay leaf
1 tsp dried thyme
400g/14oz potatoes, peeled & thinly sliced
Salt & pepper to taste

Method:

- Brown the lamb in a frying pan with some low cal cooking spray for a few minutes and place in an ovenproof dish.
- Put to one side and gently sauté the carrots and onion in the same pan for a few minutes using a little more low cal oil if needed.
- Add the flour and stir well, pour in the stock, thyme, tomato puree, bay leaf & worcestershire sauce and bring to the boil.
- Add the contents of the pan to the ovenproof dish and stir. Arrange the potato slices over the top. Season well, spray with cooking oil and cover with foil.
- Place on the lower rack of the halogen oven at 180C/350F and cook for 60-70 minutes or until the lamb is cooked through and the potato slices are tender.
- Remove the foil cover for the last 10 minutes of cooking to brown the potatoes.

Hotpot is a traditionally made with lamb/mutton and onions and almost always topped with sliced potatoes.

Herby Shepherd's Pie

Serves 4

Calories Per Serving **490**

Ingredients:

Low cal cooking oil spray
450g/1lb lean minced lamb
1 onion, chopped
2 carrots, diced
2 stalks celery, chopped
2 garlic cloves, crushed
2 tsp plain/all-purpose flour
50g/2oz mushrooms, sliced
75g/3oz peas
200g/7oz tinned chopped tomatoes
1 bay leaf
1 tsp each freshly chopped thyme, rosemary & basil
1 tbsp worcestershire sauce
120ml/ ½ cup beef stock
2 tbsp tomato purée
500g/1lb 2oz potatoes
Splash of milk
Salt & pepper to taste

Method:

- Cook the potatoes in salted boiling water until tender. Mash into a smooth consistency with a splash of milk.
- Meanwhile brown the lamb mince in a little low cal cooking oil discarding any fat which runs off.
- Remove from the pan and gently sauté the onions, celery, carrots, garlic & chopped herbs for a few minutes in the same pan before stirring through the flour.
- Add all the other ingredients, except the mashed potato, to an ovenproof dish.
- Cover and cook on the lower rack of the halogen oven at 200C/400F for 15-20 minutes.
- After this time cover evenly with the mashed potato and replace in the oven. Leave to cook for a further 10-20 minutes until the meat is cooked through, the vegetables are tender and the mash is golden brown. Increase the temperature at the end of the cooking time if needed.

Shepherd's pie was was originally known as cottage pie. People began using the term shepherds when using lamb mince rather than beef.

Stateside BBQ Sloppy Joes

Serves 4

Ingredients:

Low cal cooking oil spray
450g/1lb lean ground beef
400g/14oz tinned chopped tomatoes
1 onion, chopped
1 red (bell) pepper, chopped
1 tsp mild chilli powder
½ tsp each garlic powder, mustard powder & paprika
1 tsp soy sauce
1 tsp worcestershire sauce
2 tbsp BBQ sauce
Salt & pepper to taste
4 wholemeal soft burger rolls

390 Calories Per Serving

Method:

- Gently brown the beef in a frying pan with a little low cal cooking spray and set to one side.
- In the same pan sauté the onions and peppers for a few minutes.
- Combine all the ingredients, except the BBQ sauce, in an ovenproof dish.
- Season and cook on the lower rack of the halogen oven at 200C/400F for 20-25 minutes or until the beef is cooked through and the liquid has reduced.
- Load the mince into the soft burger rolls, add the BBQ sauce and serve.

Don't worry about getting messy - the joy is in the eating not the cleaning up!

Steak Pie, Squash & Greens

Serves 4

Calories Per Serving **399**

Ingredients:

450g/1lb lean skirt steak, trimmed & cubed
1 onion, chopped
250ml/1 cup beef stock
150g/5oz butternut squash flesh finely chopped
2 carrots, sliced
2 tsp worcestershire sauce
225g/8oz ready made low fat puff pastry
1 tsp cornflour
Splash of milk
200g/7oz spring greens, shredded
2 tsp garlic oil
Salt & pepper to taste

Steak pie is a classic family meal. The squash is this recipe adds a lovely additional depth to the dish.

Method:

- Brown the steak in a pan with a little low cal cooking spray. Remove to a plate.
- Gently sauté the onion, carrots & squash in the same pan for a few minutes.
- Put the meat back into the pan, add the stock, seasoning and worcestershire sauce. Stir and put into an ovenproof pie-dish.
- Cover and place on the lower rack of the halogen oven to cook at 180C/350F for 25-30 minutes or until the steak is cooked through.
- Place the cornflour in a cup and add a little water to create a paste.
- Add the paste to the pie dish and stir through to thicken.
- Roll out the puff pastry and cover the meat. Push the edges down and trim off the sides.
- Brush with a little milk, increase the temperature of the halogen to 200C/400F and bake for 10-15 minutes until the pastry puffs up and is golden brown. Increase the temperature at the end of cooking time if needed.
- Meanwhile steam the spring greens for a few minutes. Dress with garlic oil, season, toss & serve with the steak pie.

Toad In The Hole & Baked Beans

Serves 4

350 Calories Per Serving

Ingredients:

Low cal cooking oil spray
8 thick low-fat pork sausages
1 tsp olive oil
125g/4oz plain/all-purpose flour
2 free range eggs
250ml/1 cup semi skimmed milk
2 tsp dijon mustard
½ tsp each of dried thyme and rosemary
400g/14oz tin of baked beans
Salt & pepper to taste

Method:

- Pierce the sausages and put in an ovenproof dish with a little low cal oil. Cook on the lower rack of the halogen oven at 200C/400F for 8-12 minutes or until the sausages are browned.
- Meanwhile make up the batter by sifting the flour into a bowl. Beat the eggs into the flour and gradually add the milk, beating all the time to create a smooth batter.
- Add the dried herbs, mustard and seasoning.
- Split the cooked sausages lengthways and arrange in the ovenproof dish. Pour the batter over the top and cook for a further 25-35 minutes or until the batter is golden brown and puffed up.
- Heat the baked beans in a saucepan and serve with the toad in the hole.

Some sliced red onion in the batter is a nice addition to this dish.

Bigger Beef Quarter Pounder Burger

Serves 4

Calories Per Serving **320**

Ingredients:

Low cal cooking oil spray
500g/1lb 2oz lean beef mince
2 pieces brown bread
2 eggs
1 onion
4 garlic cloves
1 tsp each ground cumin, turmeric and paprika
3 tsp dijon mustard
2 romaine lettuce, shredded
4 ripe tomatoes, sliced
4 soft wholemeal burger rolls
Salt & pepper to taste

Method:

- Place the bread and garlic in a food processor and pulse to make breadcrumbs.
- Add the onion and whizz again.
- Add the mince, spices & eggs and pulse for a few seconds longer until combined.
- Season well and form into 4 large burger patties.
- Spray with a little low cal cooking oil and place on the grill rack at the top of the halogen oven on 240C/475F. Grill for 5-7 mins each side, or until the burgers are cooked through.
- Meanwhile gently toast the burger rolls and spread on the mustard.
- Serve with tomato and lettuce on top.

It's worth investing in a plastic burger maker to make perfect burgers shapes. They cost very little and really improve the shape and texture of the patty.

Lamb, Chickpea & Peach Casserole

Serves 4

395

Calories Per Serving

Ingredients:

Low cal cooking oil spray
400g/14oz lean lamb fillet, cubed
2 onions, chopped
2 tsp each ground cumin & coriander/cilantro
1 tsp each ground cinnamon & chilli powder
4 ripe peaches, stoned and cut into wedges
2 x 400g/14oz tins chopped tomatoes
1 x 400g/14oz tin chickpeas, drained
4 garlic cloves, crushed
3 tbsp worcestershire sauce
3 tbsp tomato puree/paste
2 tbsp freshly chopped flat leaf parsley
Salt & pepper to taste

Method:

- Gently sauté the onion, garlic & spices in a little low cal spray for a few minutes until softened.
- Add the chopped tomatoes and cubed lamb and cook for 3-4 minutes longer.
- Combine all the ingredients, except the chopped parsley, in an ovenproof dish. Place on the lower rack, cover and leave to cook in the halogen oven at 200C/400F for 40-50 minutes or until the lamb is tender and cooked through.
- Season well and serve with the chopped parsley sprinkled over the top.

Tinned peach slices will work equally well in this recipe

Cheesy Greek Moussaka

Serves 4

Calories Per Serving **390**

Ingredients:

Low cal cooking oil spray
400g/14oz lean lamb mince
4 small aubergines/egg-plants, halved and sliced
2 onions, chopped
1 tsp each ground cinnamon & all spice
2 tsp each oregano & thyme
2 x 400g/14oz tins chopped tomatoes
3 garlic cloves, crushed
500ml/2 cups fat free Greek yoghurt
200g/7oz low fat grated cheddar cheese
3 tbsp tomato puree/paste
2 tbsp freshly chopped basil
Salt & pepper to taste

Method:

- Gently sauté the onion, garlic, aubergines & spices in a little low cal oil for a few minutes until softened.
- Add the chopped tomatoes, puree & lamb mince and cook for 3-4 minutes longer.
- Place all the ingredients, except the chopped basil, yoghurt & cheese, in an ovenproof dish. Layering the aubergine slices on top.
- Meanwhile very gently heat the yoghurt and cheese together in a saucepan and, when combined, carefully pour over the top of the ovenproof dish.
- Place on the lower rack, cover and leave to cook in the halogen oven at 200C/400F for 30-40 minutes or until the lamb is tender and cooked through.
- Season well and serve with the chopped basil sprinkled over the top.

There is always a chance the yoghurt can split during cooking so be really careful when gently heating with the cheese.

Ham & Leek Bake

Serves 4

415

Calories Per Serving

Ingredients:

Low cal cooking oil spray
4 tsp low-cal 'butter' spread
4 tsp plain/all-purpose flour
500ml/2 cups semi skimmed milk
400g/14oz desiree potatoes, peeled & cubed
100g/3 ½oz grated low fat cheese
1 tbsp dijon mustard
4 leeks, sliced
50g/2oz grated cheese
400g/14oz lean cooked ham, chopped
125g/4oz fresh breadcrumbs
4 garlic cloves, crushed
4 tbsp freshly chopped parsley
300g/11oz tenderstem broccoli, roughly chopped
Salt & pepper to taste

Method:

- Gently sauté the garlic, potatoes & leek in a little low cal spray for a few minutes until softened.
- Gently heat the 'butter' in a saucepan and add the flour, stirring continuously to create a roux.
- Slowly add the milk and carry on stirring to prevent lumps. Warm through until the sauce thickens a little.
- Combine all the ingredients in an ovenproof dish and sprinkle the breadcrumbs on top. Place on the lower rack and leave to cook in the halogen oven at 200C/400F for 15-20 minutes or until the vegetables are tender.
- Season well and serve.

Make fresh breadcrumbs by placing a slice or two of brown bread in a food processor and pulsing for a few seconds.

Spaghetti & Meatballs

Serves 4

Calories Per Serving **315**

Ingredients:

Low cal cooking oil spray
400g/14oz lean beef mince
2 slices brown bread
2 free range eggs
1 onion
4 garlic cloves
2 tsp each ground cumin, turmeric, paprika & dried oregano
4 tbsp freshly chopped basil
500ml/2 cups tomato passatta/sieved tomatoes
2 tbsp worcestershire sauce
1 tsp each salt & brown sugar
225g/8oz spaghetti
Salt & pepper to taste

Method:

- Place the bread and garlic in a food processor and pulse to make breadcrumbs. Add the onions and whizz again.
- Add the mince, spices, herbs & eggs and pulse for a few seconds longer until well combined. Season and form into small meatballs with your hands.
- Place in an ovenproof dish, spray with a little low cal cooking oil and put on the lower rack in the halogen oven at 200C/400F for 10-15 minutes.
- Combine together the passatta, worcestershire sauce, salt & sugar. Add to the meatballs, mix well and continue to cook for a further 10-15 minutes until the meatballs are cooked through and the sauce is piping hot.
- Meanwhile cook the spaghetti in salted boiling water until tender. Serve with the meatballs and sauce piled on top of the spaghetti.

You could choose to sprinkle the fresh basil over the dish at the end rather than including in the meatball mix

Creamy Beef Stroganoff & Rice

Serves 4

370

Calories Per Serving

Ingredients:

Low cal cooking oil spray
450g/1lb lean sirloin steak, cut into fine strips
2 onions, chopped
2 tsp each dried oregano & tarragon
300g/11oz chestnut mushrooms, sliced
3 garlic cloves, crushed
1 tbsp dijon mustard
120ml/ ½ cup beef stock
250ml/1 cup low fat crème fraiche
200g/7oz long grain rice
2 tbsp freshly chopped flat leaf parsley
Salt & pepper to taste

Method:

- Gently sauté the onions, garlic & mushrooms in a little low cal oil for a few minutes.
- Add the steak and cook for 3-4 minutes longer.
- Place all the ingredients, except the rice, in an ovenproof dish and combine well.
- Place on the lower rack, cover and leave to cook in the halogen oven at 200C/400F for 10-15 minutes or until the sauce is creamy & the steak is tender and cooked through (add a little more crème fraiche or stock if needed).
- Meanwhile cook the rice in salted boiling water until tender.
- Season well and serve with the stroganoff piled on top of a bed of rice.

Cut the steak as thinly as possible. Try putting it in the freezer for half an hour before slicing and you'll find it easier to cut finely.

Spanish Sausage Casserole

Serves 4

370

Calories Per Serving

Ingredients:

Low cal cooking oil spray
200g/7oz lean pork sausages, sliced
200g/7oz uncooked chorizo sausages, sliced
2 onions, chopped
4 yellow (bell) peppers, sliced
3 tsp each mixed dried herbs & smoked paprika
2 x 400g/14oz tins chopped tomatoes
1 x 400g/14 oz tin mixed beans, drained
4 garlic cloves, crushed
2 tbsp worcestershire sauce
3 tbsp tomato puree/paste
Salt & pepper to taste

Method:

- Gently sauté the onion, sliced peppers, garlic & herbs in a little low cal oil for a few minutes until softened.
- Add the sausages and chorizo and cook for 3-4 minutes longer.
- Combine all the ingredients in an ovenproof dish. Place on the lower rack and leave to cook in the halogen oven at 200C/400F for 25-30 minutes or until the sausages are cooked through and the beans are tender.
- Season well and serve.

Use uncooked chorizo sausage for this dish rather than the salami style cured chorizo.

Pork Loin Steaks & Apple

Serves 4

320 Calories Per Serving

Ingredients:

Low cal cooking oil spray
4 pork loin steaks – each weighing 125g/4oz
250ml/1 cup pure apple juice
4 golden delicious apples (or similar), peeled & chopped
8 garlic cloves, crushed
300g/11oz mushrooms, sliced
120ml/½ cup low fat crème fraiche
300g/11oz shredded vegetable ribbons
Salt & pepper to taste

Method:

- Season the pork loin steaks. Spray with a little low cal cooking oil and place in an ovenproof dish on the grill pan at the top of the halogen oven at 240C/475F. Grill for 3-4 mins each side.
- Meanwhile gently sauté the chopped apples, garlic and mushrooms in a little low cal oil for a few minutes until softened.
- Stir through the apple juice & crème fraiche and pour over the pork steaks (use the same pan for the vegetables later).
- Reduce the heat in the halogen oven to 200C/400F and cook for a further 6-8 minutes or until the pork is cooked through.
- Meanwhile use the same pan to gently sauté the vegetable ribbons for a few minutes in any leftover juices from the mushroom mixture.

Pan-ready shredded vegetables are widely available and really useful to have in.

Pork Tenderloin & Orange

Serves 4

Calories Per Serving **295**

Ingredients:

Low cal cooking oil spray
500g/1lb 2oz piece pork tenderloin
120ml/½ cup chicken stock
120ml/½ cup fresh orange juice
4 garlic cloves, crushed
4 tbsp freshly chopped sage
300g/11oz butternut squash, peeled & cut into thin chips or small cubes
200g/7oz spinach, chopped
Salt & pepper to taste

Method:

- Season the pork tenderloin. Spray with a little low cal cooking oil and quickly brown in a frying pan for a few minutes.
- Place in an ovenproof dish with all the other ingredients and cover tightly. Cook on the lower rack of the halogen oven at 200C/400F for 30-40 minutes or until the pork is cooked through and the squash is tender.
- Remove the pork and cut into thick slices.
- Arrange on the plate with the spinach and squash to the side.
- Pour the juices over the top of the pork and vegetables and serve.

Root vegetables can take longer to cook than meat so ensure the squash is cut into small enough pieces so that it is tender once the pork is ready.

Chocolate Chilli Beef

Serves 4

375

Calories Per Serving

Ingredients:

Low cal cooking oil spray
500g/1lb 2oz lean minced beef
2 tsp each ground cumin & mild chilli powder
1 ½ tbsp cocoa powder
1 tsp ground allspice
4 carrots, cut into batons
2 onions, chopped
200g/7oz ripe tomatoes, chopped
4 garlic cloves, crushed
1 tbsp dried basil
2 tbsp sundried tomato paste
250ml/1 cup beef stock
8 taco shells
4 tbsp fat free Greek yoghurt
2 baby gem lettuce, shredded
Salt & pepper to taste

Method:

- Gently sauté the onion, garlic, spices & herbs in a little low cal spray for a few minutes until softened.
- Add all the other ingredients and cook for 4-5 minutes longer.
- Combine all the ingredients, except the yoghurt, lettuce & taco shells, in an ovenproof dish.
- Place on the lower rack and leave to cook in the halogen oven at 200C/400F for 20-25 minutes or until the mince is cooked through and the stock is absorbed.
- Season well and serve with the taco shells, shredded lettuce and yoghurt.

The cocoa powder in this recipe gives a lovely chocolate sweetness which is always a hit.

Lamb & Chapatti Bread

Serves 4

Calories Per Serving **390**

Ingredients:

Low cal cooking oil spray
450g/1lb lean minced lamb
4 tbsp balsamic vinegar
1 tsp each garam masala, ground turmeric, coriander/cilantro
4 garlic cloves, crushed
6 carrots, chopped
2 red onions, chopped
1 tbsp mint sauce
120ml/½ cup lamb or chicken stock
4 chapatti bread wraps
Salt & pepper to taste

Method:

- Season the lamb, spray with a little low cal cooking oil and quickly brown in a frying pan for a few minutes.
- Place in an ovenproof dish with all the other ingredients, except the chapatti bread.
- Cook on the lower rack of the halogen oven at 200C/400F for 20-25 minutes or until the lamb is cooked through and the carrots are tender.
- Serve with the chapatti bread on the side.

Chapatti is a widely available light Indian bread which you will find in most supermarkets.

Mini Lamb Burgers

Serves 4

390

Calories Per Serving

Ingredients:

Low cal cooking oil spray
500g/1lb 2oz lean lamb mince
2 tsp each ground coriander, garlic, salt, paprika, cumin & turmeric
2 onions, very finely chopped
1 green chilli, very finely chopped
3 tbsp freshly chopped mint
2 tbsp lemon juice
4 pitta bread
2 romaine lettuces, shredded
4 ripe tomatoes, finely chopped
Salt & pepper to taste

Method:

- Gently sauté the onion, green chilli, salt, coriander, paprika, cumin, turmeric and garlic in a little low cal cooking oil for a few minutes.
- Place the mince, lemon juice, chopped mint and warm spicy onion mixture into a food processor and whizz together.
- Take the mixture out, divide into 20-24 portions and shape into small flat meat patties.
- Spray with a little low cal cooking oil and place on the grill rack at the top of the halogen oven on 240C/475F. Grill for 4-5 minutes each side or until the lamb is properly cooked through.
- Serve inside the pitta bread with the lettuce and tomatoes.

This is a traditional Asian dish which is known as Shami Tikka in Indian cooking.

Honey Pork Noodles

Serves 4

Calories Per Serving 420

Ingredients:

Low cal cooking oil spray
500ml/1lb 2oz pork tenderloin, cubed
2 onions, chopped
4 garlic cloves, crushed
4 tsp runny honey
1 tbsp soy sauce
1 tbsp tomato puree/paste
250ml/1 cup chicken stock
2 tsp sesame seeds
1 large bunch chopped spring onions/scallions
2 pak choi, shredded
2 limes, cut into wedges
225g/8oz fine egg noodles
Salt & pepper to taste

Method:

- Season the pork, spray with a little low cal cooking oil and quickly brown in a frying pan for a few minutes.
- Place in an ovenproof dish with all the other ingredients, except the sesame seeds, spring onions, lime wedges and noodles. Cover tightly and cook on the lower rack of the halogen oven at 200C/400F for 20-25 minutes or until the pork is cooked through.
- Meanwhile cook the noodles in boiling salted water until tender.
- When the pork is cooked, season and serve on a bed of noodles with the sesame seeds & spring onions sprinkled over the top and lime wedges on the side.

Pour any leftover juices from the ovenproof dish over the top of the pork and noodles.

Gnocchi & Sausage Bake

Serves 4

395 Calories Per Serving

Ingredients:

Low cal cooking oil spray
8 lean pork sausages, sliced
2 onions, chopped
3 tbsp worcestershire sauce
250ml/1 cup passata/ sieved tomatoes
2 tsp dried rosemary
1 tsp brown sugar
½ tsp salt
400g/14oz tinned chopped tomatoes
200g/7oz fresh spinach
500g/1lb 2oz gnocchi

Method:

- Gently brown the onion and sliced sausages in a little low cal cooking oil for a few minutes.
- Place in an ovenproof dish with all the ingredients and mix well. Cover and cook on the lower rack of the halogen oven at 200C/400F for 20-25 minutes or until the sausages are cooked through and the gnocchi dumplings are tender.

Use the salt & sugar carefully to balance the acidity of the tomatoes in this dish.

Chorizo Omelette

Serves 4

Calories Per Serving **240**

Ingredients:

Low cal cooking oil spray
4 onions
500g/1lb 2oz potatoes, leave unpeeled
4 free range eggs
75g/3oz thinly sliced cured chorizo sausage, chopped
200g/7oz mixed salad leaves
Salt & pepper to taste

Method:

- In a food processor whizz together the potatoes and onion.
- Gently sauté in a little low cal oil for 5-10 minutes until softened.
- Beat the eggs and combine with the sautéed mixture in a shallow greased ovenproof dish.
- Season well, place on the lower rack and cook in the halogen oven at 200C/400F for 25-35 minutes or until the omelette is firm.
- Cut into wedges and serve with mixed salad leaves on the side.

If your family are not a fan of chorizo you can use any chopped salami type meat.

THE Skinny HALOGEN OVEN FAMILY FAVOURITES RECIPE BOOK

Poultry

Chicken Korma

Serves 4

Calories Per Serving **410**

Ingredients:

Low cal cooking oil spray
500g/1lb 2oz skinless chicken breast, cubed
370ml/1 ½ cups tomato passata/sieved tomatoes
1 onion, finely chopped
½ tsp salt
1 tsp brown sugar
1 tbsp mild curry powder
1 tbsp ground almonds
3 tbsp tomato puree/paste
1 tsp each ground garlic, cumin, garam masala, coriander/cilantro & turmeric powder
60ml/ ¼ cup coconut milk
200g/7oz basmati rice

Method:

- Brown the meat for a few minutes in a frying pan with a little low cal spray.
- Add the dried spices, curry powder, onions & tomato puree and gently cook for a minute or two.
- Put in an ovenproof dish and add the tomato passata, sugar, salt and ground almonds.
- Place on the lower rack and leave to cook in the halogen oven at 200C/400F for 15-20 minutes or until the chicken is cooked through.
- Meanwhile rinse the rice in a sieve with cold water and cook in a pan of salted boiling water until tender.
- Stir the coconut milk through the curry and serve with the rice.

Korma is a mild family curry which usually always contains coconuts and/or almonds. This version contains both!

Chicken Biryani

Serves 4

420

Calories Per Serving

Ingredients:

Low cal cooking oil spray
400g/14oz skinless chicken breast, cubed
370ml/1 ½ cups tomato passata/sieved tomatoes
1 onion, finely chopped
2 carrots, finely chopped
1 tbsp mild curry powder
½ tsp salt
1 tsp brown sugar
3 tbsp tomato puree/paste
75g/3ozfrozen peas
½ tsp each ground garlic, cumin, coriander, paprika & turmeric powder
3 tbsp fat free Greek yoghurt

Rice Ingredients:

200g/7oz basmati rice
½ onion, finely chopped
¼ tsp ground cinnamon
¼ tsp ground cloves
1 bay leaf
Pinch of Saffron
1 chicken stock cube
2 tsp sunflower oil

Method:

- Brown the meat for a few minutes in a frying pan with a little low cal spray. Add the dried spices, curry powder, onions, carrots and tomato puree and gently cook for a minute or two.
- Put in an ovenproof dish and add the tomato passata, peas, sugar & salt. Place on the lower rack and leave to cook in the halogen oven at 200C/400F for 15-20 minutes or until the chicken is cooked through.
- Meanwhile rinse the rice in a sieve with cold water. Boil a pan of water and dissolve the cube of chicken stock into it. Gently fry the onion, cinnamon and cloves for a few minutes in the sunflower oil.
- Add the rice to the onion mix and coat well, transfer contents of frying pan plus the bay leaf and saffron into the boiling stock water and cook until tender.
- When both the rice and curry are ready, stir the yoghurt through the curry. Combine the rice and curry together to make a delicious biryani.

This version of biryani prepares both rice and sauce separately before combining at the end. Alter spice quantities to suit your taste.

Chicken Goujons

Serves 4

450

Calories Per Serving

Ingredients:

Low cal cooking oil spray
3 slices white bread
1 clove garlic
½ tsp paprika
25g/1oz grated parmesan cheese
500g/1lb 2oz skinless chicken breasts, cut into strips
50g/2oz plain/all-purpose flour
2 free range eggs
Salt & pepper to taste
125g/4oz peas
4 wholemeal soft rolls
1 tbsp low fat mayonnaise
1 lemon cut into wedges

Method:

- First make the breadcrumbs: put the bread, paprika, garlic, cheese and a pinch of salt and pepper into a food processor and whizz until you have breadcrumbs.
- Sieve the flour onto a plate. Put the breadcrumbs on a separate plate and beat the eggs in a bowl.
- Cover each chicken strip with flour by rolling them on the flour plate and then dip each strip in the egg. Finally coat well in breadcrumbs.
- Spray with low cal cooking oil and place on a grill pan at the bottom of the halogen oven on 200C/400F for 10-15 minutes or until the chicken is cooked through and the goujons are golden brown – increase the temperature if necessary.
- Meanwhile cook the peas in boiling water until tender. Split the rolls and spread with mayonnaise. Serve the golden goujons with peas, rolls and lemon wedges on the side.

Homemade chicken goujons are a healthy alternative to shop bought chicken nuggets.

Chicken Fajitas

Serves 4

390 Calories Per Serving

Ingredients:

Low cal cooking oil spray
400g/14oz skinless chicken breasts, sliced into strips
60ml/¼ cup chicken stock
1 onion, sliced
3 red & yellow (bell) peppers, sliced
2 tbsp lime juice
4 flour tortilla wraps
1 romaine lettuce shredded
2 vine ripened tomatoes, chopped
4 tbsp fat free Greek yoghurt
Salt & pepper to taste

Fajita Spice Mix Ingredients:

1 tsp mild chilli powder
½ tsp each ground cumin, paprika, onion powder, garlic powder & dried oregano
Pinch crushed chilli flakes

Method:

- Combine the fajita spice mix and lime juice together and mix well with the chicken strips. Season, cover and leave to chill for an hour or two.
- Meanwhile sauté the onion & peppers in a little low cal cooking oil for a few minutes.
- Add all the ingredients, except the flour tortillas, salad & yoghurt into an ovenproof dish. Place on the lower rack of the halogen oven and cook at 200C/400F for 20-30 minutes or until the chicken is cooked through.
- Spoon the chicken and pepper mix into flour tortillas.
- Add the yoghurt and salad. Fold & enjoy.

Of course you may prefer a spicier fajita, so add additional fresh chillies or chilli powder to suit your taste.

Triple Cheese Lasagne

Serves 4

Calories Per Serving **450**

Ingredients:

Low cal cooking spray
1 onion, chopped
3 garlic cloves, crushed
400g/14oz tinned chopped tomatoes
2 tbsp tomato puree/paste
2 tsp dried mixed herbs
1 tbsp worcestershire sauce
½ tsp salt
400g/14oz lean minced turkey
75g/3oz low fat ricotta cheese
50g/2oz low fat mozzarella cheese, grated
2 free range eggs, beaten
50g/2oz low fat cheddar, grated
150g/5oz fresh lasagne sheets

Method:

- Gently sauté the turkey mince, onion and garlic in a little low cal oil for a few minutes.
- Add the chopped tomatoes, puree, salt & worcestershire sauce and cook for 4-5 minutes.
- Meanwhile mix the ricotta, mozzarella and eggs together. In an ovenproof dish layer in turn the lasagne sheets, meat and cheese mixes, finishing with a layer of meat on top sprinkled with the grated cheddar cheese.
- Place on the lower rack of the halogen oven, cover with foil and cook at 200C/400F for 30-40 minutes or until cooked through.
- Remove the foil for the last 10 minutes of cooking to brown the cheese.

Using turkey mix is a great low fat alternative to the traditional beef mince recipe.

Lemon & Tarragon Chicken Breasts

Serves 4

240

Calories Per Serving

Ingredients:

4 skinless chicken breasts - each weighing 125g/4oz
4 garlic cloves, crushed
4 tsp freshly chopped tarragon
4 lemons
1 tsp crushed chilli flakes
200g/7oz rocket leaves
60g/2½oz parmesan shavings
Salt & pepper to taste

Method:

- Chop two of the lemons into slices. Squeeze and reserve the juice from the other two.
- Combine the lemon juice, garlic, tarragon and chilli flakes together to create a marinade.
- Place the chicken breasts in an ovenproof dish and score the flesh of each with a knife. Brush the breasts evenly with all the marinade, season well and leave for up to 1 hour to marinate.
- Carefully cover the chicken breasts with the sliced lemon pieces, place on the lower rack and leave to cook in the halogen oven for 25-30 minutes at 200C/400F or until the chicken breasts are cooked through.
- Remove the cooked chicken to four plates and serve with the rocket salad and parmesan shavings.

If there is any marinade left in the bowl after cooking, spoon it onto the salad as a dressing.

Caribbean Chicken With Rice & Sweet Potato

Serves 4

Calories Per Serving **390**

Ingredients:

Low cal cooking oil spray
1 onion, chopped
4 skinless chicken breasts - each weighing 125g/4oz
300g/11oz sweet potato, peeled & thinly sliced
3 tsp plain/all-purpose flour
4 garlic cloves, crushed
2 tsp each cayenne pepper, paprika & mustard seeds
4 tsp freshly grated ginger
1 tsp ground cinnamon
250ml/1 cup chicken stock
250ml/1 cup low fat coconut milk
175g/6oz long grain rice
Salt & pepper to taste

Method:

- Gently sauté the onion, garlic, dried spices and mustard seeds in a little low-cal spray for a few minutes until the onion softens and the mustard seeds begin to pop.
- Stir through the flour and add the hot chicken stock to the pan. Continue stirring for a minute or two.
- Combine all the ingredients, except the coconut milk, in an ovenproof dish. Place on the lower rack and leave to cook in the halogen oven at 180C/350F for 30-35 minutes or until the chicken is cooked through and the sweet potato is tender.
- Meanwhile cook the rice in salted boiling water until tender.
- When the chicken is cooked gently stir through the coconut milk and cut the breasts into thick diagonal slices.
- Season, serve with the boiled rice and pour all the coconut juices over the dish.

You could try using plantain in this dish rather than sweet potato for an authentic West Indian touch

310

Calories Per Serving

Red Pesto Chicken & Green Beans

Serves 4

Ingredients:

Low cal cooking oil spray
4 skinless chicken breasts - each weighing 125g/4oz
2 onions, sliced
4 tsp red pesto
4 tsp dried oregano
2 red onions, sliced into rounds
200g/7oz French beans
200g/7oz baby sweetcorn
Salt & pepper to taste

Method:

- Hold each breast and slice through the centre. Stop slicing before you cut in half completely and open up to 'butterfly' it.
- Open the chicken breast to expose the two inside parts. Spread the inside with 1 tsp pesto and close your 'sandwich' back up so you are left with pesto through the centre of each chicken breast.
- Place the chicken breasts, onions and vegetables in an ovenproof dish. Season well, sprinkle with dried oregano and spray with a little low-cal cooking oil.
- Place on the lower rack and leave to cook in the halogen oven at 200C/400F for 25-30 minutes or until the chicken is cooked through and the vegetables are tender.
- Remove from the halogen oven and arrange the beans, corn and onions as a bed onto which you serve the pesto chicken breast.

You may need to cover the dish during cooking if the vegetables are browning too quickly.

Creamy Mint Chicken & New Potatoes

Serves 4

350

Calories Per Serving

Ingredients:

Low cal cooking oil spray
4 skinless chicken breasts - each weighing 125g/4oz
2 onions, chopped
1 tbsp dijon mustard
250ml/1 cup low fat crème fraiche
200g/7oz small new potatoes/halved
200g/7oz spinach leaves
200g/7oz chestnut mushrooms, sliced
250ml/ 1 cup chicken stock
1 tbsp freshly chopped mint
Salt & pepper to taste

Method:

- Slice the chicken breasts into strips.
- Gently sauté the onion and mushrooms in a little low cal oil for a few minutes.
- Add the chicken stock and mustard to the pan and bring to the boil. Continue stirring for a minute or two while it bubbles away.
- Combine all the ingredients, except the crème fraiche and chopped mint, in an ovenproof dish. Place on the lower rack and leave to cook in the halogen oven at 180C/350F for 20-25 minutes or until the chicken is cooked through and the potatoes are tender.
- After cooking gently stir through the crème fraiche, season and serve with the chopped mint sprinkled over the top.

You could alter this recipe by changing the chopped mint to chopped parsley or oregano if you prefer.

Mild Paprika Chicken & Chorizo

Serves 4

410 Calories Per Serving

Ingredients:

Low cal cooking oil spray
500g/1lb 2oz skinless chicken breast meat, sliced
2 onions, chopped
3 tsp smoked paprika
2 tsp dried sage
2 tbsp freshly chopped basil leaves
2 x 400g/14oz tins chopped tomatoes
1 yellow (bell) pepper, sliced
200g/7oz uncooked chorizo sausage, sliced
4 garlic cloves, crushed
50g/2oz pitted olives, halved
200g/7oz purple sprouting broccoli, roughly chopped
Salt & pepper to taste

Method:

- Gently sauté the onion, sliced pepper, garlic & paprika in a little low cal oil for a few minutes until softened.
- Add the sliced chorizo & chicken and cook for 3-4 minutes longer.
- Combine all the ingredients, except the fresh chopped basil, in an oven-proof dish. Place on the lower rack and leave to cook in the halogen oven at 200C/400F for 25-30 minutes or until the chicken is cooked through and the vegetables are tender.
- Season well and serve.

If purple sprouting broccoli is not in season feel free to use spinach or any other green leaf vegetable to give the dish additional goodness.

Cream Cheese Chicken & Ham

Serves 4

Calories Per Serving 330

Ingredients:

4 skinless chicken breasts - each weighing 125g/4oz
4 tbsp low fat cream cheese with herbs
4 slices parma ham
300g/11oz ripe tomatoes, halved
300g/11oz spinach or spring greens
1 tbsp garlic oil
Salt & pepper to taste

Method:

- Make a lengthways slit in each chicken breast and stuff with the cream cheese.
- Season and wrap with a slice of parma ham (secure in place with a dampened cocktail stick skewered through the breast).
- Place in an ovenproof dish on the lower rack and leave to cook in the halogen oven at 200C/400F for 25-30 minutes or until the chicken is cooked through.
- Meanwhile mix together the halved tomatoes, garlic oil and spinach leaves so that they all have a thin coating of oil on them.
- Season well and place around the chicken breasts in the casserole dish 10 minutes before the end of cooking time.
- Arrange and serve in a shallow bowl.

You could use any type of thin cured meat to wrap the chicken breast in, or whichever soft cheese and herb variety you prefer.

Laughing Cow Creamy Chicken

Serves 4

360

Calories Per Serving

Ingredients:

4 skinless chicken breasts - each weighing 125g/4oz
4 tbsp light Laughing Cow soft cheese
3 tbsp sundried tomato paste
300g/11oz mixed baby vegetables
Salt & pepper to taste

Method:

- First cut the chicken breasts. Hold each breast as if you were slicing through the centre to butterfly it. Stop slicing before you cut it in half completely and open to expose the two inside parts.
- Spread the inside of each chicken breast with soft cheese and close your 'sandwich' back up.
- Spread the top with the sundried tomato paste and cover all the breasts with foil.
- Place in an ovenproof dish on the lower rack and leave to cook in the halogen oven at 200C/400F for 25-30 minutes or until the chicken is cooked through.
- Meanwhile steam the baby vegetables over a pan of boiling water for 5-10 minutes or until tender.
- Season well and serve with the chicken.

Laughing Cow is a brand of mild soft cheese sold widely in the US and UK. Substitute for any other soft cheese you wish.

Nutty Chicken & Mushrooms

Serves 4

Calories Per Serving **390**

Ingredients:

4 skinless chicken breasts - each weighing 125g/4oz
2 tsp ground almonds
60g/2½oz plain cashew nuts, finely chopped
200g/7oz mushrooms, finely chopped
2 onions, finely chopped
4 tsp garlic paste
300g/11oz new potatoes
Salt & pepper to taste

Method:

- First mix together the ground almonds, cashews, mushrooms, onion & garlic paste.
- Make a lengthways slit in each chicken breast and stuff with the walnut mixture. Don't worry if it's overflowing just gently wrap each breast in foil to keep it together.
- Place in an ovenproof dish on the lower rack and leave to cook in the halogen oven at 200C/400F for 30-35 minutes or until the chicken is cooked through.
- Meanwhile steam the new potatoes over a pan of boiling water for 10-20 minutes or until tender.
- Season well and serve with the chicken breast.

Cashews are a favourite nut but you could opt for peanuts or walnuts if you like.

Spiced Chicken Kebabs
Serves 4

260

Calories Per Serving

Ingredients:

500g/1lb 2oz skinless chicken breast meat, cubed
4 tbsp fat free Greek yoghurt
2 tsp each ground cumin, turmeric, coriander/ cilantro & mild chilli powder
3 garlic cloves, crushed
8 metal skewers
4 baby gem lettuce, shredded
2 red onions, sliced
2 lemons cut into wedges
Salt & pepper to taste

Method:

- Season the cubed chicken.
- Mix together the spices, garlic & yoghurt and add the chicken. Combine well, cover and leave to chill for an hour or two.
- Skewer the chicken pieces to make 8 chicken kebabs and place on the grill rack at the top of the halogen oven on 240C/475F.
- Grill for 6-8 minutes each side or until the chicken is cooked through (take care handling the skewers as they will get hot).
- Serve with the shredded lettuce, sliced onions and lemon wedges.

Marinating the chicken for this Indian spiced dish is preferable but not essential

Butter Bean Chicken Stew

Serves 4

390

Calories Per Serving

Ingredients:

Low cal cooking oil spray
500g/1lb 2oz skinless chicken breast meat, sliced
2 onions, chopped
2 tsp each dried oregano, basil & rosemary
200g/7oz tinned chopped tomatoes
200g/7oz tinned butter beans, drained
2 yellow (bell) peppers, sliced
3 garlic clove, crushed
3 tbsp worcestershire sauce
3 tbsp tomato puree/paste
Salt & pepper to taste

Method:

- Gently sauté the onion, sliced pepper, garlic & herbs in a little low cal oil for a few minutes until softened.
- Add the chopped tomatoes and sliced chicken and cook for 3-4 minutes longer.
- Combine all the ingredients in an ovenproof dish.
- Place on the lower rack and leave to cook in the halogen oven at 200C/400F for 25-30 minutes or until the chicken is cooked through and the vegetables are tender.
- Season well and serve.

Butter beans are some of the most popular of all legumes. They are also known as lima beans.

Lean Turkey & Onion Burger

Serves 4

280 Calories Per Serving

Ingredients:

Low cal cooking oil spray
500g/1lb 2oz lean turkey mince
2 pieces brown bread
2 free range eggs
2 onions
3 garlic cloves
1 tbsp fat free mayonnaise
1 iceberg lettuce, shredded
2 ripe tomatoes, sliced
4 wholemeal brown soft burger rolls
Salt & pepper to taste

Method:

- Place the bread and garlic in a food processor and pulse to make breadcrumbs. Add the onion and whizz again.
- Add the turkey mince & eggs and pulse for a few seconds longer until combined.
- Season well and form into 4 large burger patties by working into 4 balls and then shaping with your hands into 2cm/1 inch thick discs.
- Spray with a little low cal cooking oil and place on the grill rack at the top of the halogen oven on 240C/475F. Grill for 5-7 minutes each side, or until the burgers are cooked through.
- Spread the mayonnaise on each split burger bun and serve with sliced tomatoes and shredded lettuce on top.

It's worth investing in a plastic burger-maker. They cost very little and really improve the shape and texture of the meat patty.

Indian Chicken & Minted Yoghurt
Serves 4

Calories Per Serving

295

Ingredients:

Low cal cooking oil spray
4 skinless chicken breasts - each weighing 125g/4oz
2 tsp each ground cumin, turmeric, coriander/cilantro & chilli powder
1 tsp each ground ginger, paprika & garam masala
4 tbsp lemon juice
5 garlic cloves, crushed
3 baby gem lettuce, shredded
2 red onions, sliced
2 lemons cut into wedges
250ml/1 cup fat free Greek yoghurt
4 tsp mint sauce
Salt & pepper to taste

Method:

- Mix together the lemon juice, ground spices & garlic to form a paste (add a little water if needed).
- Season the chicken breasts and spray with a little low cal oil. Score the chicken breasts all over with a knife and smother them in the spice paste.
- Place in an ovenproof dish and leave for up to 1 hour to marinate.
- Place on the lower rack and leave to cook in the halogen oven for 25-30 minutes at 200C/400F or until the chicken is cooked through.
- Meanwhile mix the mint sauce and Greek yoghurt together.
- Plate up the chicken breasts with the lettuce & onion and serve the lemon wedges and mint yoghurt on the side.

Shop-bought mint sauce is a great 'cheat' ingredient for making Indian condiments

Sweet Runny Honey Chicken

Serves 4

310 Calories Per Serving

Ingredients:

Low cal cooking oil spray
500g/1lb 2oz skinless chicken breast meat, cubed
300g/11oz sweet potatoes, cubed
3 parsnips, cubed
4 carrots, sliced
2 onions, sliced
250g/9oz vine-ripened tomatoes, halved
4 garlic cloves, crushed
4 tbsp lemon juice
4 tsp soy sauce
2 tbsp runny honey
Salt & pepper to taste

Method:

- Mix together the garlic, lemon juice, honey and soy sauce.
- Brush the chicken, tomatoes & vegetables with the honey mixture.
- Place the vegetables in an ovenproof dish. Season and spray with a little low cal oil.
- Cover and place on the lower rack of the halogen oven for 20 minutes.
- Add the chicken and tomatoes to the dish and cook for a further 15-20 minutes or until the chicken is cooked through and the vegetables are tender.

Honey and chicken is a lovely combination. You could serve this with some pitta bread

Cinnamon Chicken & Saffron Rice

Serves 4

Calories Per Serving **310**

Ingredients:

4 skinless chicken breasts - each weighing 125g/4oz
1 ½ tsp ground cinnamon
1 tsp each paprika, cumin & coriander/cilantro
½ tsp nutmeg
4 garlic cloves, crushed
200g/7oz basmati rice
200g/7oz peas
Pinch saffron
Salt & pepper to taste

Method:

- Mix the ground spices and garlic together with a little water to form a paste.
- Score the chicken breasts with a knife and smother each in the spice paste.
- Place on the lower rack, cover with foil and leave to cook in the halogen oven at 200C/400F for 25-30 minutes, or until the chicken is cooked through.
- Meanwhile cook the rice and peas separately in salted boiling water.
- Add a pinch of saffron to the pan of rice and serve with the chicken.

Saffron is a delicate spice which is actually taken from a flower known as the Saffron Crocus.

Smothered Peanut Butter Chicken

Serves 4

320

Calories Per Serving

Ingredients:

4 skinless chicken breasts - each weighing 125g/4oz
4 red (bell) peppers, sliced
2 onions, chopped
4 tbsp low fat smooth peanut butter
4 tbsp lime juice
250ml/1 cup chicken stock
4 tsp soy sauce
2 tsp each, paprika, ground cumin & coriander/cilantro
200g/7oz boiled long grain rice
Salt & pepper to taste

Method:

- Mix the ground spices and peanut butter together to form a paste.
- Score the chicken breasts with a knife and smother in the spice paste.
- Add all the ingredients to an ovenproof dish and cover. Place on the lower rack and leave to cook in the halogen oven at 200C/400F for 25-30 minutes or until the chicken is cooked through.
- Meanwhile cook the rice in salted boiling water until tender.
- Slice the chicken breast into thick slices, place on top of the rice and pour the peppers and stock over the top of the chicken.

Use smooth peanut butter rather than the crunchy variety for this recipe.

Parmesan Chicken & Farfalle
Serves 4

Calories Per Serving **340**

Ingredients:

200g/7oz farfalle pasta
4 tsp green pesto
4 skinless chicken breasts - each weighing 125g/4oz
2 tbsp low fat mayonnaise
2 tbsp parmesan cheese, grated

Method:

- Boil the pasta in salted water until tender.
- Drain, mix with the pesto and leave to cool.
- Meanwhile combine the mayonnaise & parmesan together and smother over the chicken breasts.
- Place in an ovenproof dish on the lower rack and cook in the halogen oven at 200C/400F for 25-30 minutes or until the chicken is cooked through.
- Serve with the cooled pesto pasta on the side.

Any grated hard cheese will work well with this recipe.

Sweet Chicken & Salad Wrap

Serves 4

350

Calories Per Serving

Ingredients:

500g/1lb 2oz skinless chicken breast meat, cubed
3 garlic cloves, crushed
3 tbsp soy sauce
1 tbsp runny honey
1 tbsp tomato puree/paste
½ tsp each mustard powder & ground ginger
120ml/½ cup chicken stock
1 iceberg lettuce, chopped
4 low fat soft tortilla wraps
4 ripe tomatoes, chopped
4 tbsp low fat crème fraiche
Salt & pepper to taste

Method:

- Mix together the stock, garlic, soy sauce, honey, tomato puree and ground spices.
- Place the chicken pieces in an ovenproof dish and combine well with the honey and stock mixture.
- Season well, cover and place on the lower rack of the halogen oven. Leave to cook for 15-20 minutes at 200C/400F or until the chicken is cooked through.
- Serve the chicken pieces in each tortilla wrap with the lettuce, tomatoes and cream fraiche.

This sweet wrap is great as a cold lunch as well as a hot wrap.

THE *Skinny* OVEN
HALOGEN
FAMILY FAVOURITES
RECIPE BOOK

Vegetarian

Macaroni Cheese

Serves 4

Calories Per Serving **280**

Ingredients:

300g/11oz macaroni pasta
1 tbsp dijon mustard
250ml/1 cup low fat crème fraiche
6 tbsp milk
½ tsp nutmeg
200g/7oz grated mature cheddar cheese (or vegetarian alternative)
100g/3½oz spinach, chopped
6 vine ripened tomatoes, chopped
Salt & pepper to taste

Method:

- Cook the pasta in salted boiling water until tender.
- Meanwhile gently warm through the mustard, crème fraiche, milk, nutmeg and cheese in a saucepan.
- Combine all the ingredients in an ovenproof dish. Season well, cover and place on the lower rack of the halogen oven. Leave to cook for 25-30 minutes at 200C/400F or until piping hot.

Wholegrain mustard is also good in this recipe. You could substitute some steamed tenderstem broccoli in place of the spinach.

Double Cheese Family Pizza

Serves 4

420

Calories Per Serving

Ingredients:

1 packet yeast
125g/4oz whole-wheat flour
125g/4oz plain/all-purpose flour
3 tsp runny honey
½ salt
½ tbsp extra virgin olive oil
180ml/ ¾ cup warm water

Topping Ingredients:

(Use vegetarian cheese alternatives as required)
Low cal cooking oil spray
4 tbsp tomato puree
2 tsp garlic paste
2 tbsp grated parmesan
200g/7oz low fat mozzarella cheese, cubed
Salt and pepper to taste
1 bunch chopped basil

Method:

- Place the yeast, water and honey in a mixer. Leave to stand for a minute. Start mixing and slowly add the flour.
- Add the olive oil & salt and mix into a dough. When the dough is formed take out and bring together into one ball. Place back in the bowl and cover with clingfilm.
- Leave to rest for 30 mins or until the dough has increased to double its size. Cut in two and roll into two 25-30cm pizzas on pieces of baking parchment.
- Mix the tomato and garlic purees together and spread onto the dough discs. Arrange the cubed mozzarella evenly over the two dough discs and spray with oil.
- Leave to cook at 200C/400F or about 8-10 minutes, or until the bases are properly cooked and the topping is bubbling. Use both racks for the 2 bases. Swapping around half way through cooking.
- Remove from the oven and sprinkle with fresh parmesan and basil.

This simple recipe makes two 25-30cm/11 inch pizzas. Experiment with toppings to suit your families' taste.

Mixed Bean Chilli
Serves 4

Calories Per Serving **305**

Ingredients:

Low cal cooking oil spray
3 onions, chopped
2 x 400g/14oz tins chopped tomatoes
2 x 400g/14oz tins mixed beans
3 tbsp tomato puree/paste
100g/3 ½oz chestnut mushrooms, sliced
3 carrots, chopped
1 tsp each ground cumin, paprika & coriander/cilantro
3 garlic cloves, crushed
2 tsp brown sugar
1 tbsp freshly chives
Salt & pepper to taste

Method:

- Gently sauté the onion, garlic and mushroom in a little low cal oil until softened.
- Combine all the ingredients, except the chopped chives, in an ovenproof dish.
- Season well, cover and place on the lower rack of the halogen oven. Leave to cook for 30-35 minutes at 200C/400F or until piping hot.
- Sprinkle with chopped chives and serve.

Tinned mixed beans are a really useful store cupboard ingredient to have around.

Sweet & Sour Vegetables & Noodles

Serves 4

275 Calories Per Serving

Ingredients:

Low fat cooking oil spray
3 mixed colours red (bell) peppers, sliced
1 red onion, cut into edges
3 tbsp soy sauce
2 tbsp tomato puree/paste
1 tbsp cider/white wine vinegar
2 tsp cornflour
4 tbsp water
75g/3 oz baby corn
75g/5oz sugarsnap peas
200g/7oz ready to go shredded vegetables & beansprouts
2 garlic cloves, crushed
125g/4oz tinned pineapple chunks
120ml/ ½ cup pineapple juice
1 tsp brown sugar
125g/4oz egg noodles

Method:

- Add the garlic, vegetables, pineapple chunks, juice, soy, sugar, vinegar and puree to an ovenproof dish.
- Mix well, cover and leave to cook on the bottom rack of the halogen oven on 200C/400F for 10-20 minutes or until the vegetables are tender.
- Meanwhile mix together the corn-flour and water to form a paste (use a little more water if needed).
- Cook the noodles in salted boiling water until tender.
- Once the vegetables are cooked stir through the cornflour paste to thicken the sauce.
- Leave to cook for a minute or two longer and serve with the noodles.

To get the sweet and sour balance right you might need to adjust the sugar and cider vinegar quantities.

THE *Skinny* OVEN
HALOGEN
FAMILY FAVOURITES
RECIPE BOOK

Fish & Seafood

Homemade Fish Fingers With Ketchup Mayo

Serves 4

350

Calories Per Serving

Ingredients:

Low cal cooking oil spray
1 free range egg
1 tbsp plain/all-purpose flour
75g/3oz breadcrumbs
1 lemon
400g/14oz skinless, boneless cod or haddock fillets
2 tbsp low fat mayonnaise
1 tbsp ketchup
1 tsp dried basil
125g/4oz peas
1 tsp grated parmesan cheese
Salt & pepper to taste

These homemade fish fingers are always popular with the whole family.

Method:

- First slice the fish fillets into strips.
- Make the breadcrumbs by putting a piece of bread and a pinch of salt and pepper into a food processor and pulse until you have breadcrumbs.
- Sieve the flour onto a plate. Put the breadcrumbs on a separate plate and beat the egg in a bowl.
- Cover each fish strip with flour by rolling them on the flour plate and then dip each strip in the egg.
- Finally coat well in the breadcrumbs.
- Spray with low cal cooking oil and place on a grill pan at the bottom of the halogen oven on 200C/400F for 10-15 minutes or until the fish is cooked through and the breadcrumbs are golden brown – increase the temperature if necessary.
- Meanwhile cook the peas in salted boiling water and sprinkle over the parmesan when cooked and drained. Mix the ketchup and mayonnaise together in a small bowl for dipping. Cut the lemon into wedges and serve with the fish fingers & peas.

Salmon Fish Pie

Serves 4

470 Calories Per Serving

Ingredients:

225g/8oz boneless salmon fillets
225g/8oz boneless haddock fillets
800g/1lb 11oz desiree potatoes, peeled and cubed
100g/3½oz peas
100g/3½oz sweetcorn
100g/3½ oz low fat cheddar cheese, grated
1 carrot, finely chopped
25g/1oz low fat 'butter' spread
1 tbsp plain/all-purpose flour
2 cups skimmed milk
1 tsp dijon mustard

Method:

- Place the fish in a pan and cover with milk. Gently poach for 8-10 minutes until the fish is cooked and flakes easily with a fork.
- Remove the fish from the pan and reserve the milk.
- Place the cooked fish, sweetcorn, carrots & peas in an ovenproof dish.
- Meanwhile, cook the potatoes in salted boiling water until tender. When they are ready, drain and mash using a splash of the fishy milk.
- Gently melt the low fat spread in a pan and stir through the flour. When you have made a roux (paste) begin adding the reserved fishy milk and continue stirring. The sauce will thicken after a minute or two.
- Add the mustard and cheese, remove from the heat and pour onto the fish and vegetables in the ovenproof dish.
- Cover with the smooth mash, place on the lower rack of the halogen oven and cook at 200C/400F for 20-30 minutes or until the vegetables are tender.

Feel free to use alternative fish in this recipe. Any meaty white fish is good with the salmon.

Lemon Sole Gratin

Serves 4

285

Calories Per Serving

Ingredients:

Low cal cooking oil spray
4 boneless lemon sole fillets - each weighing 125g/4oz
4 garlic cloves, crushed
2 onions, chopped
100g/3½oz fresh breadcrumbs
1 tbsp grated parmesan cheese
4 tbsp freshly chopped flat leaf parsley
200g/7oz chestnut mushrooms, chopped
8 vine ripened tomatoes
1 tbsp anchovy paste
200g/7oz rocket leaves
2 lemons cut into wedges
Salt & pepper to taste

Method:

- Slice each lemon sole fillet to create a cavity for stuffing.
- Gently sauté the mushrooms, garlic, onions & anchovy paste together in a little low cal oil for a few minutes.
- Stuff this mixture equally into each fillet.
- Mix together the breadcrumbs, parmesan and chopped parsley.
- Place the stuffed fillet and tomatoes on the grill pan of the halogen oven, season and sprinkle with the breadcrumb mix.
- Cook for 8-12 minutes at 240C/475F or until the fish is properly cooked through.
- Serve with the rocket salad and lemon wedges.

Make fresh breadcrumbs by placing a slice or two of brown bread in a food processor and pulsing for a few seconds.

Salmon Pesto Fillets & Sweet Potatoes

Serves 4

355

Calories Per Serving

Ingredients:

4 thick skinless, boneless salmon fillets - each weighing 125g/4oz
3 tbsp green pesto
100g/3½ oz fresh breadcrumbs
1 tbsp grated parmesan cheese
500g/1lb 2oz sweet potato, peeled & cubed
200g/7oz mangetout
Salt & pepper to taste

Method:

- Mix together the breadcrumbs, parmesan & pesto and spread evenly over the top of the salmon fillets.
- Place the salmon on the grill pan at the top of the halogen oven and cook for 8-12 minutes at 240C/475F or until the salmon is properly cooked through.
- Meanwhile boil the sweet potato for 10 minutes or until tender. Season well and mash a little with the back of a fork.
- Steam the mangetout for a few minutes on top of the boiling pan while the potatoes are cooking.
- Arrange the vegetables and fish together on a plate and serve.

Shop-bought pesto in a jar is fine for this recipe but you could try making your own too.

Sweet Soy Salmon

Serves 4

260

Calories Per Serving

Ingredients:

4 thick skinless, boneless salmon fillets - each weighing 125g/4oz
4 tsp runny honey
2 tbsp soy sauce
2 tsp sesame oil
2 lemons cut into wedges
300g/11oz asparagus spears
50g/2oz gruyere cheese, grated
Salt & pepper to taste

Method:

- Mix together the honey, soy sauce and sesame oil.
- Place the salmon fillets and asparagus on an ovenproof dish at the top of the halogen oven and brush with the honey mix. Cook for 8-12 minutes at 240C/475F or until the salmon fillets are cooked through and the asparagus spears are tender.
- Sprinkle the cheese over the asparagus to melt 2-3 mins before the end of cooking.
- Serve with lemon wedges on the side.

Cheddar cheese rather than gruyere cheese will work just as well.

Fresh Tuna Steaks

Serves 4

270 Calories Per Serving

Ingredients:

4 thick boneless tuna fillets – each weighing 125g/4oz
2 tbsp balsamic vinegar
2 tbsp soy sauce
2 tsp chilli oil
500g/1lb 2oz beansprout & vegetable mix
Salt & pepper to taste

Method:

- Mix together the balsamic vinegar, soy sauce and chilli oil.
- Place the tuna fillets on the grill pan at the top of the halogen oven and brush with the balsamic/oil mix. Cook for 6-10 minutes at 240C/475F or until the tuna is cooked to your preference (6 minutes of cooking will leave it quite rare).
- Meanwhile use the rest of the balsamic/oil mix to stir-fry the beansprouts for a few minutes while the tuna cooks in the halogen oven.
- Add a little more soy sauce to the beansprouts during cooking if needed.
- Serve the tuna steak on top of the stir-fried beansprouts and vegetables.

Bags of fresh beansprouts and shredded vegetables are available almost everywhere and are really quick and easy to use. Leave out the chilli oil if it's too spicy for your family.

Tuna & Noodle Casserole
Serves 4

Calories Per Serving **310**

Ingredients:

Low cal cooking oil spray
3 onions, chopped
500g/1lb 2oz tinned tuna, drained
200g/7oz peas
300g/11oz fine egg noodles
400g/14oz tins chopped tomatoes
1 tsp crushed chilli flakes
3 tbsp sundried tomato paste
Salt & pepper to taste

Method:

- Gently sauté the onion in a little low cal spray for a few minutes until soft.
- Cook the noodles in salted boiling water until tender.
- Combine all the ingredients really well in an ovenproof dish.
- Season, place on the lower rack and leave to cook in the halogen oven at 200C/400F for 20-25 minutes or until piping hot.

You could use pasta rather than noodles if you prefer.

Tasty King Prawn Kebabs

Serves 4

260 Calories Per Serving

Ingredients:

Low cal cooking oil spray
500g/1lb 2oz large raw king prawns
½ tsp each ground cumin, turmeric, paprika & coriander/cilantro
2 tsp brown sugar
3 tbsp lemon juice
3 garlic cloves, crushed
4 baby gem lettuce, shredded
4 orange (bell) peppers, cut into pieces
2 lemons cut into wedges
250ml/1 cup fat free Greek yoghurt
3 tsp mint sauce
12 metal skewers
Salt & pepper to taste

Method:

- Mix together the lemon juice, ground spices & garlic to form a paste (add a little water if needed).
- Season the prawns and pepper pieces, spray with a little low cal oil and smother in the spice paste.
- Place in a dish and leave for up to 1 hour to marinate.
- Skewer the prawns and pepper pieces in turn to make 10-12 kebabs.
- Place on the grill rack at the top of the halogen oven on 240C/475F. Grill for 4-6 minutes each side or until the prawns are cooked through and the pepper pieces are tender (take care handling the skewers as they will get hot).
- Meanwhile mix the mint sauce and Greek yoghurt together. Plate up the skewers along with the shredded lettuce and serve the lemon wedges and mint yoghurt on the side.

You could substitute the sweet peppers for mushrooms, tomatoes, babycorn or whatever your family prefers.

Creamy Fish & Prawn Bake

Serves 4

375

Calories Per Serving

Ingredients:

125g/4oz fresh breadcrumbs
300g/11oz small peeled prawns
300g/11oz boneless white fish fillet, cut into chunks
200g/7oz spinach, chopped
200g/7oz tenderstem broccoli, roughly chopped
200g/7oz sweetcorn
250ml/1 cup milk
4 tbsp low fat soft cream cheese
2 lemons cut into wedges
Salt & pepper to taste

Method:

- Gently heat the milk and cream cheese in a saucepan to make a creamy sauce.
- Carefully combine all the ingredients in an ovenproof dish, season and sprinkle the breadcrumbs on top.
- Place on the lower rack and leave to cook in the halogen oven at 200C/400F for 30-35 minutes or until the seafood is properly cooked through and the vegetables are tender.
- Serve with lemon wedges on the side.

Any type of meaty white fish fillets will work well with this recipe.

Haddock & Tomato Stew

Serves 4

220 Calories Per Serving

Ingredients:

300g/7oz small peeled prawns
300g/7oz boneless, skinless haddock fillets, cut into chunks
3 onions, chopped
3 garlic cloves, crushed
120ml/½ cup fish or chicken stock
500g/1lb 2oz fresh tomatoes, finely chopped
3 tsp anchovy paste
1 tbsp sundried tomato paste
1 tbsp each freshly chopped basil
2 bay leaves
Salt & pepper to taste

Method:

- Gently sauté the onion, anchovy paste & garlic in a little low cal oil for a few minutes.
- Add all the ingredients to an oven-proof dish and season well.
- Cover with foil, place on the lower rack and leave to cook in the halogen oven at 180C/350F for 30-35 minutes or until the seafood is properly cooked through.

It's fine to use tinned tomatoes if you don't have fresh tomatoes to hand.

Pollack & Peanut Butter

Serves 4

Calories Per Serving **420**

Ingredients:

4 boneless, skinless pollack fillets – each weighing 125g/4oz
2 tbsp peanut butter
3 tbsp soy sauce
2 tbsp freshly chopped coriander/cilantro
6 large vine ripened tomatoes, sliced
2 red onions sliced into rounds
400g/14oz tinned kidney beans, drained
Salt & pepper to taste

Method:

- Mix together the peanut butter paste, soy sauce and 1 tbsp of the chopped coriander.
- Place the pollack fillet on the grill pan at the top of the halogen oven and brush over the peanut butter & herb mixture. Cook for 8-12 minutes at 240C/475F or until the fish is properly cooked through.
- Meanwhile arrange the kidney beans, sliced tomatoes and onion slices on a plate.
- Scatter the remaining chopped coriander over the top.
- Season and serve with the cooked pollack fillet.

The kidney bean salad may not be overly popular if you are feeding children, so consider making baked potatoes in the halogen as an accompaniment for them instead.

Sardines, Sultanas & Potato Salad

Serves 4

395 Calories Per Serving

Ingredients:

Low cal cooking oil spray
900g/2lb whole fresh sardines, gutted and cleaned
3 garlic cloves, crushed
2 onions, chopped
100g/3½oz fresh breadcrumbs
1 tbsp freshly chopped flat leaf parsley
2 tbsp sultanas, chopped
500g/1lb 2oz salad potatoes, halved
1 small bunch spring onions/scallions, chopped.
1 tbsp low-fat mayonnaise
2 lemons cut into wedges
Salt & pepper to taste

Method:

- First make a simple potato salad by boiling the potatoes in salted water until tender.
- Season well, leave to cool and mix with the mayonnaise & spring onions.
- Gently sauté the garlic, breadcrumbs & sultanas in a little low cal oil for a few minutes until softened.
- Stuff the breadcrumb/sultana mix into the whole sardines and place on the grill pan of the halogen oven. Season and cook for 8-12 minutes at 240C/475F or until the sardines are properly cooked through.
- Sprinkle chopped parsley over the top and serve with the potato salad and lemon wedges at the side.

Fresh sardines can be surprising well received by youngsters who love seeing the whole fish cooked.

Monk Fish & Fries

Serves 4

420

Calories Per Serving

Ingredients:

Low cal cooking oil spray
4 skinless, boneless monkfish fillets – each weighing 125g/4oz
3 orange (bell) peppers, sliced
2 red onions, sliced
1 tbsp freshly chopped basil
4 tbsp lime juice
125g/4oz Salad leaves
Salt & pepper to taste

Fries Ingredients:

Low cal cooking spray
600g/1lb 5oz sweet potatoes, peeled
2 tsp brown sugar
1 tsp crushed sea salt
1 tsp paprika

Method:

- Combine the monkfish, peppers and onions with the lime juice and leave to marinate for a few minutes.
- Prepare and cook the fries (see page 86)
- Season, place on a grill tray at the top of the halogen oven and cook for 8-12 minutes at 240C/475F or until the fish is properly cooked through and the vegetables are tender.
- Serve the monkfish and vegetables with the fries and salad leaves on the side.

The lime juice not only marinates the monkfish it also begins to 'cook' the fillet so don't leave it to marinate for too long.

THE *Skinny* OVEN
HALOGEN
FAMILY FAVOURITES
RECIPE BOOK

Sides

Paprika Sweet Potato French Fries

Serves 4

Calories Per Serving **190**

Ingredients:

Low cal cooking spray
600g/1lb 5oz sweet potatoes, peeled
2 tsp brown sugar
1 tsp crushed sea salt
1 tsp paprika

Method:

• Cut the potatoes into thin slices and then in rows to make thin French fries, keeping them all a similar size.
• Put the raw fries into a bowl and coat with paprika, low-cal cooking oil, salt and sugar. Mix really well to make sure they are properly covered.
• Spread them out onto a baking tray on the lower rack and leave to cook in the halogen oven at 200C/400F for 15-20 or until tender.
• After this time move the fries to the upper shelf and increase the heat to brown the fries if needed.

When you cook the fries don't pile them up, they should be set out in a thin layer so that they can cook evenly.

Baked Potatoes

Serves 4

160

Calories Per Serving

Ingredients:

Low cal cooking oil spray
2 tsp crushed sea salt
4 baking potatoes – each weighing 125g/4oz
Salt & pepper to taste

Method:

- Spray the potatoes with a little low cal oil, pierce with a fork and use your hands to rub in the oil and crushed salt.
- Place on the lower grill rack and leave to cook in the halogen oven at 200C/400F for 50-60 minutes or until tender.
- Cut in half, season well and serve.

Serve as a side dish to a meal or stuff with your favourite filling. Good low fat family favourites include cottage cheese, tuna & sweetcorn and baked beans.

Garlicky Sweet Potato

Serves 4

Calories Per Serving 155

Ingredients:

Low cal cooking oil spray
2 tsp crushed sea salt
4 sweet potatoes, each weighing 150g/5oz
4 garlic cloves, unpeeled
Salt & pepper to taste

Method:

- Spray the potatoes and garlic cloves with a little low cal oil, pierce with a fork and use your hands to rub the oil and crushed salt into the skins.
- Place on the lower grill rack and leave to cook in the halogen oven at 200C/400F for 50-60 minutes or until tender.
- Cut the potatoes in half and scoop out the flesh.
- Squeeze the garlic cloves out of their skins and mash with a fork.
- Mix the garlic and soft potato flesh together, season and serve.

You can also serve as a traditional baked potato, rather than a mash, by loading the mixed garlic and potato flesh back into the empty skins.

Cauliflower Cheese

Serves 4

140 Calories Per Serving

Ingredients:

2 cauliflowers, broken into florets
2 onions, chopped
100g/3½oz breadcrumbs
4 tbsp low fat cream cheese
8 tbsp milk
Salt & pepper to taste

Method:

- Steam the cauliflower florets until tender.
- Meanwhile gently heat together the cream cheese, onions and milk.
- Place the cauliflower in an ovenproof dish and pour over the cream cheese sauce.
- Season well and sprinkle on breadcrumbs.
- Place on the lower rack and leave to cook in the halogen oven at 240C/475F for 5-10 minutes or until golden brown.

This is quite a big side dish, so consider portion size when you are serving as part of a meal.

Sunshine Rice

Serves 4

Calories Per Serving **190**

Ingredients:

Low cal cooking oil spray
300g/11 oz basmati rice
750ml/3 cups vegetable stock
2 onions, chopped
2 bay leaves
3 tsp turmeric
Salt & pepper to taste

Method:

- Gently sauté the onion in a little low cal cooking oil.
- Add all the ingredients to the pan and bring to the boil.
- Transfer to an ovenproof dish and cover.
- Place on the lower rack and leave to cook in the halogen oven at 200C/400F for 25-35 minutes or until the rice is tender.Add a little more stock if needed.
- Remove the bay leaf, drain, season and serve.

The turmeric in this dish gives it a really strong yellow colour, hence its name 'sunshine rice'.

Potato Wedges

Serves 4

160 Calories Per Serving

Ingredients:

Low cal cooking oil spray
2 tsp crushed sea salt
500g/1lb 2oz desiree potatoes
2 garlic cloves, crushed
Salt & pepper to taste

Method:

- Leave the potatoes unpeeled and cut into wedges.
- Spray with a little low cal oil and combine the salt and garlic well with the potato wedges.
- Place on a baking tray in a single layer on the lower rack and leave to cook in the halogen oven at 220C/450F for 25-35 minutes or until golden & tender.

Desiree potatoes are ideal for this recipe but any potato should do well. Try adding some dried basil & rosemary with the garlic if you like.

THE Skinny HALOGEN OVEN FAMILY FAVOURITES RECIPE BOOK

Snacks

Pepperoni Pitta Snack Pizza

Serves 4

Calories Per Serving **260**

Ingredients:

Low cal cooking oil spray
2 wholemeal pitta bread
4 tbsp tomato puree/paste
4 vine ripened tomatoes, chopped
1 onion, sliced
125g/4oz low fat cheddar cheese, grated
2 tbsp freshly chopped basil leaves
50g/2oz pepperoni slices
1 iceberg lettuce, shredded
Salt & pepper to taste

Method:

- Slice the pitta breads lengthways in half to make 4 pitta pizza bases.
- Spread the tomato puree over each pitta base.
- Arrange the tomatoes, onion, cheese, basil and pepperoni slices on the top.
- Spray with a little low cal cooking oil and place on the top grill rack of the halogen oven at 220C/425F. Grill for 8-10 minutes or until the pizzas are cooked through.
- Serve with shredded lettuce on the side.

This is a really handy snack-meal which you can put together in no time at all.

Marmite Cheese On Toast

Serves 4

160 Calories Per Serving

Ingredients:

4 slices wholegrain bread
125g/4oz grated cheddar cheese
1 tsp marmite (or more to taste)
Salt & pepper to taste

Method:

- Gently spread the marmite over the bread slices.
- Sprinkle with cheese, season and place on the top grill rack of the halogen oven.
- Cook at 240C/475F for 4-5 minutes or until brown and bubbling.

You could alter this recipe by not using marmite and mixing the grated cheese with worcestershire sauce instead.

Tomato & Cheese Ciabatta

Serves 4

Calories Per Serving **180**

Ingredients:

Low cal cooking oil spray
4 slices ciabatta bread
125g/4oz grated cheddar cheese
8 cherry tomatoes, sliced
4 tsp tomato puree/paste
4 tsp basil leaves, chopped
Salt & pepper to taste

Method:

- Spread the puree on the ciabatta slices.
- Lay the cheese and sliced cherry tomatoes on top.
- Season, spray with a little oil and place on the top grill rack of the halogen oven. Cook at 240C/475F for 4-5 minutes or until the cheese is melted.
- Sprinkle with basil leaves and serve.

This is a simple and quick 'open' sandwich which is also good with sundried tomato paste.

Ham & Cheese Panini

Serves 4

290

Calories Per Serving

Ingredients:

4 paninis sliced
4 slices gouda cheese
4 slices lean cured ham
Salt & pepper to taste

Method:

- Place the cheese and ham inside the paninis.
- Season and place on the top grill rack of the halogen oven.
- Cook at 240C/475F for 4-5 minutes or until brown and bubbling.
- Turn once during cooking.

You can use any filling you prefer for your panini. There are endless possibilities and your halogen oven will cook them super-quick.

Eggy Rarebit Muffin

Serves 4

Calories Per Serving **295**

Ingredients:

4 breakfast muffins, split in two halves
4 tsp plain/all-purpose flour
60ml/¼ cup milk
4 free range eggs
125g/4oz mature cheddar, grated,
2 tsp dijon mustard

Method:

- Heat the milk in a pan and whisk in the flour.
- Take off the heat and mix in the cheese, eggs and mustard.
- Pile on top of the breakfast muffin halves.
- Season and place on the top grill rack of the halogen oven. Cook at 240C/475F for 4-5 minutes or until brown and bubbling.

You could add some chopped ham or herbs to this if you like.

THE *Skinny* HALOGEN OVEN
FAMILY FAVOURITES
RECIPE BOOK

Desserts

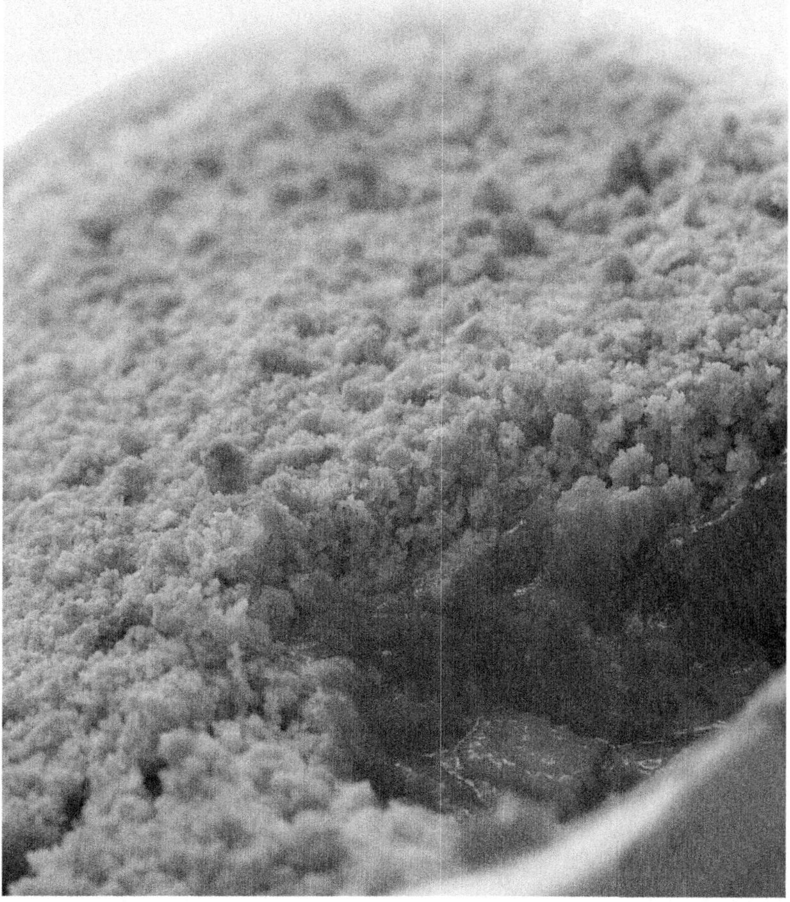

Sticky Golden Syrup Pudding

Serves 4

Calories Per Serving 390

Ingredients:

Low cal cooking oil spray
100g/3½oz low fat 'butter' spread
100g/3½oz brown sugar
100g/3½oz self raising flour, sieved
2 free range eggs
4 tbsp golden syrup
1 tsp runny honey

Method:

- First cream together the butter and sugar before adding the eggs and flour until the pudding mixture is smooth.
- Use a little low cal spray to grease a small ovenproof dish. Add the honey and syrup to the bottom of the dish and pour the pudding mixture on top.
- Place on the lower rack and leave to cook in the halogen oven for 20-25 minutes at 220C/425F or until the pudding has risen and is cooked through.

You could add some fat free Greek yoghurt to serve if you wish.

Blackberry Crumble

Serves 4

320 Calories Per Serving

Ingredients:

600g/1lb 5oz ripe blackberries
3 tbsp sugar
2 tbsp water
1 tbsp golden syrup
2 tsp water
200g/7oz oats
60ml/¼ cup milk
50g/2oz low fat 'butter' spread, melted

Method:

- Mix together the sugar, water and blackberries. Put in an ovenproof dish and pour any juices over the top.
- Place on the lower rack and leave to cook in the halogen oven for 8-10 minutes at 200C/400F.
- Meanwhile mix together the syrup, oats & melted butter and spread on top of the cooking soft fruit.
- Return to the oven and leave to cook for a further 14-18 minutes.
- Serve with the milk poured over the top.

You may need to adjust the temperature to make sure the crumble on top doesn't burn.

Sliced Peaches & Vanilla Yoghurt

Calories Per Serving **290**

Serves 4

Ingredients:

2 x 400g/14oz tins sliced peaches
1 tbsp brown sugar
½ tsp vanilla extract
2 cups fat free Greek vanilla yoghurt
Pinch nutmeg

Method:

- Mix together the sugar, vanilla extract and peach slices.
- Place in an ovenproof dish on the lower rack of the halogen oven for 10-12 minutes at 200C/400F.
- Gently stir through the yoghurt and serve immediately with a pinch of nutmeg.

The vanilla extract and vanilla yoghurt work really well together in this dish.

Baked Apple & Sultanas

Serves 4

295 Calories Per Serving

Ingredients:

4 large cooking apples, cored (not peeled)
4 tbsp sultanas
4 tsp brown sugar
4 tbsp warm water
1 tsp each ground nutmeg & cinnamon
4 tsp runny honey
4 tbsp crème fraiche

Method:

- Mix together the honey, sugar, water, sultanas and spices.
- Stuff the mixture into the cored apples, place in an ovenproof dish and pour any juices over the top.
- Cover, place on the lower rack and leave to cook in the halogen oven for 20-30 minutes at 200C/400F or until the apples are tender.
- Serve with crème fraiche dolloped on top of each apple.

You could use ice cream rather than crème fraiche if you prefer.

Honey Bananas & Yoghurt

Serves 4

Calories Per Serving **260**

Ingredients:

8 ripe bananas, sliced
2 tbsp runny honey
2 tbsp fat free Greek yoghurt
Pinch ground cinnamon

Method:

- Place the bananas in an ovenproof dish and brush all over with the honey.
- Cover, place on the lower rack and leave to cook in the halogen oven for 10-15 minutes at 220C/450F.
- Serve with the Greek yoghurt on top sprinkled with ground cinnamon.

This is also good with ice cream or vanilla yoghurt.

Calorie Conscious

There is endless calorie information available for free online. It's almost impossible to put together a comprehensive resource as part of a book and so the list below is intended as nothing more than a guide to some of the more popular fruit, salad and vegetables to help you get a handle on food calories. All food calories are listed per 100g of the stated food.

Vegetables & Salad		**Fruit**	
Asparagus	20 cals	Apples	52 cals
Benasprouts	30 cals	Avacado	160 cals
Broccoli	34 cals	Banana	89 cals
Brussel Sprouts	42 cals	Blackberries	43 cals
Butternut Squash	45 cals	Blueberries	57 cals
Carotts	41 cals	Cantaloupe Melon	34 cals
Cauliflower	25 cals	Cherries	63 cals
Celery	14 cals	Grapefruit	32 cals
Courgette/Zucchini	16 cals	Grapes	69 cals
Cucumber	15 cals	Kiwi	61 cals
Frozen Peas	64 cals	Oranges	47 cals
Green Peas	81 cals	Peaches (canned)	44 cals
Green Pepper	20 cals	Peaches	39 cals
Leeks	61 cals	Pears	58 cals
Mixed Salad	17 cals	Pineapple	48 cals
Mushrooms	22 cals	Plums	46 cals
Pak Choi	13 cals	Raspeberries	52 cals
Parsnips	67 cals	Strawberries	32 cals
Potatoes	75 cals	Watermelon	30 cals
Red Cabbage	31 cals		
Savoy Cabbage	27 cals		
Spinach	23 cals		
Sweet Potato	86 cals		
Sweetcorn	86 cals		
Tomatoes	18 cals		
Wild Rocket	17 cals		

CONVERSION CHART: DRY INGREDIENTS

Metric	Imperial
7g	¼ oz
15g	½ oz
20g	¾ oz
25g	1 oz
40g	1½oz
50g	2oz
60g	2½oz
75g	3oz
100g	3½oz
125g	4oz
140g	4½oz
150g	5oz
165g	5½oz
175g	6oz
200g	7oz
225g	8oz
250g	9oz
275g	10oz
300g	11oz
350g	12oz
375g	13oz
400g	14oz

Metric	Imperial
425g	15oz
450g	1lb
500g	1lb 2oz
550g	1¼lb
600g	1lb 5oz
650g	1lb 7oz
675g	1½lb
700g	1lb 9oz
750g	1lb 11oz
800g	1¾lb
900g	2lb
1kg	2¼lb
1.1kg	2½lb
1.25kg	2¾lb
1.35kg	3lb
1.5kg	3lb 6oz
1.8kg	4lb
2kg	4½lb
2.25kg	5lb
2.5kg	5½lb
2.75kg	6lb

CONVERSION CHART: LIQUID MEASURES

Metric	Imperial	US
25ml	1fl oz	
60ml	2fl oz	¼ cup
75ml	2½ fl oz	
100ml	3½fl oz	
120ml	4fl oz	½ cup
150ml	5fl oz	
175ml	6fl oz	
200ml	7fl oz	
250ml	8½ fl oz	1 cup
300ml	10½ fl oz	
360ml	12½ fl oz	
400ml	14fl oz	
450ml	15½ fl oz	
600ml	1 pint	
750ml	1¼ pint	3 cups
1 litre	1½ pints	4 cups

Other
COOKNATION TITLES

If you enjoyed 'The Skinny Halogen Oven Family Favourites Recipe Book' e'd really appreciate your feedback. Reviews help others decide if this is the right book for them so a moment of your time would be appreciated.

Thank you.

You may also be interested in other '**Skinny**' titles in the CookNation series. You can find all the following great titles by searching under '**CookNation'**.

The Skinny Slow Cooker Recipe Book
Delicious Recipes Under 300, 400 And 500 Calories.

Paperback / eBook

More Skinny Slow Cooker Recipes
75 More Delicious Recipes Under 300, 400 & 500 Calories.

Paperback / eBook

The Skinny Slow Cooker Curry Recipe Book
Low Calorie Curries From Around The World

Paperback / eBook

The Skinny Slow Cooker Soup Recipe Book
Simple, Healthy & Delicious Low Calorie Soup Recipes For Your Slow Cooker. All Under 100, 200 & 300 Calories.

Paperback / eBook

The Skinny Slow Cooker Vegetarian Recipe Book
40 Delicious Recipes Under 200, 300 And 400 Calories.

Paperback / eBook

The Skinny 5:2 Slow Cooker Recipe Book
Skinny Slow Cooker Recipe And Menu Ideas Under 100, 200, 300 & 400 Calories For Your 5:2 Diet.

Paperback / eBook

The Skinny 5:2 Curry Recipe Book
Spice Up Your Fast Days With Simple Low Calorie Curries, Snacks, Soups, Salads & Sides Under 200, 300 & 400 Calories

Paperback / eBook

The Skinny Halogen Oven Family Favourites Recipe Book
Healthy, Low Calorie Family Meal-Time Halogen Oven Recipes Under 300, 400 and 500 Calories

Paperback / eBook

Skinny Halogen Oven Cooking For One
Single Serving, Healthy, Low Calorie Halogen Oven Recipes Under 200, 300 and 400 Calories

Paperback / eBook

Skinny Winter Warmers Recipe Book
Soups, Stews, Casseroles & One Pot Meals Under 300, 400 & 500 Calories.

Paperback / eBook

The Skinny Soup Maker Recipe Book

Delicious Low Calorie, Healthy and Simple Soup Recipes Under 100, 200 and 300 Calories. Perfect For Any Diet and Weight Loss Plan.

Paperback / eBook

The Skinny Bread Machine Recipe Book

70 Simple, Lower Calorie, Healthy Breads...Baked To Perfection In Your Bread Maker.

Paperback / eBook

The Skinny Indian Takeaway Recipe Book

Authentic British Indian Restaurant Dishes Under 300, 400 And 500 Calories. The Secret To Low Calorie Indian Takeaway Food At Home

Paperback / eBook

The Skinny Juice Diet Recipe Book

5lbs, 5 Days. The Ultimate Kick-Start Diet and Detox Plan to Lose Weight & Feel Great!

Paperback / eBook

Available only on eBook

The Skinny 5:2 Diet Recipe Book Collection

All The 5:2 Fast Diet Recipes You'll Ever Need. All Under 100, 200, 300, 400 And 500 Calories

eBook

The Skinny 5:2 Fast Diet Meals For One

Single Serving Fast Day Recipes & Snacks Under 100, 200 & 300 Calories

Paperback / eBook

The Skinny 5:2 Fast Diet Vegetarian Meals For One

Single Serving Fast Day Recipes & Snacks Under 100, 200 & 300 Calories

Paperback / eBook

The Skinny 5:2 Fast Diet Family Favourites Recipe Book

Eat With All The Family On Your Diet Fasting Days

Paperback / eBook

Available only on eBook

The Skinny 5:2 Fast Diet Family Favorites Recipe Book **U.S.A. EDITION**

Dine With All The Family On Your Diet Fasting Days

Paperback / eBook

The Skinny 5:2 Diet Chicken Dishes Recipe Book

Delicious Low Calorie Chicken Dishes Under 300, 400 & 500 Calories

Paperback / eBook

The Skinny 5:2 Bikini Diet Recipe Book

Recipes & Meal Planners Under 100, 200 & 300 Calories. Get Ready For Summer & Lose Weight...FAST!

Paperback / eBook

Available only on eBook

The Paleo Diet For Beginners Slow Cooker Recipe Book

Gluten Free, Everyday Essential Slow Cooker Paleo Recipes For Beginners

eBook

The Paleo Diet For Beginners Meals For One

The Ultimate Paleo Single Serving Cookbook

Paperback / eBook

Available only on eBook

The Paleo Diet For Beginners Holidays

Thanksgiving, Christmas & New Year Paleo Friendly Recipes

eBook

Available only on eBook

The Healthy Kids Smoothie Book

40 Delicious Goodness In A Glass Recipes for Happy Kids.

eBook

The Skinny Slow Cooker Summer Recipe Book

Fresh & Seasonal Summer Recipes For Your Slow Cooker. All Under 300, 400 And 500 Calories.

Paperback / eBook

The Skinny ActiFry Cookbook

Guilt-free and Delicious ActiFry Recipe Ideas: Discover The Healthier Way to Fry!

Paperback / eBook

The Skinny 15 Minute Meals Recipe Book

Delicious, Nutritious & Super-Fast Meals in 15 Minutes Or Less. All Under 300, 400 & 500 Calories.

Paperback / eBook

The Skinny Mediterranean Recipe Book

Simple, Healthy & Delicious Low Calorie Mediterranean Diet Dishes. All Under 200, 300 & 400 Calories.

Paperback / eBook

The Skinny Hot Air Fryer Cookbook

Delicious & Simple Meals For Your Hot Air Fryer: Discover The Healthier Way To Fry.

Paperback / eBook

The Skinny Ice Cream Maker

Delicious Lower Fat, Lower Calorie Ice Cream, Frozen Yogurt & Sorbet Recipes For Your Ice Cream Maker

Paperback / eBook

The Skinny Low Calorie Recipe Book

Great Tasting, Simple & Healthy Meals Under 300, 400 & 500 Calories. Perfect For Any Calorie Controlled Diet.

Paperback / eBook

The Skinny Takeaway Recipe Book

Healthier Versions Of Your Fast Food Favourites: Chinese, Indian, Pizza, Burgers, Southern Style Chicken, Mexican & More. All Under 300, 400 & 500 Calories

Paperback / eBook

The Skinny Nutribullet Recipe Book

80+ Delicious & Nutritious Healthy Smoothie Recipes. Burn Fat, Lose Weight and Feel Great!

Paperback / eBook

The Skinny Nutribullet Soup Recipe Book

Delicious, Quick & Easy, Single Serving Soups & Pasta Sauces For Your Nutribullet. All Under 100, 200, 300 & 400 Calories.

Paperback / eBook

Printed in Great Britain
by Amazon

61467425R00068